the Bread & Butter
CHRONICLES

STARSYS PUBLISHING COMPANY

The Bread & Butter Chronicles

Published by Starsys Publishing Company
526 North Alvernon Way
Tucson, Arizona 85711

This novel (excluding the Appendix) is a work of fiction. Names, characters, places, and incidents either are the product of the author's imagination or are used fictitiously. Any resemblance to actual events, locales, organizations, or persons living or dead is entirely coincidental and beyond the intent of either the author or the publisher.

This publication is designed by the author to provide information of a general nature in regard to the subject matter covered. It is not intended to provide specific professional services or advice to the reader.

Starsys Publishing Company is not responsible for and makes no representations or warrants regarding the contents of this book or the opinions expressed herein, or for the application or consequences thereof. The publisher is not engaged in rendering legal, financial, accounting, or other professional service or advice.

If legal, financial, accounting, or other professional advice or assistance is required, the author and publisher recommend that the services of a qualified professional should be sought. The author and publisher specifically disclaim any responsibility for any liability, loss or risk personally or otherwise, which is incurred as a consequence, directly or indirectly as a result of the use or application (or lack thereof) of any of the information or contents contained in this book.

ISBN 10: 0-9826622-2-X
ISBN 13: 978-0-9826622-2-9

Library of Congress Cataloging-in-publication Data pending

First printing August, 2010
Printed in the United States of America

For my husband, Brad. For believing in me and loving me thirty years and counting.

For my friend, Kerrie Droban. If not for your encouragement and enthusiasm, this book would have never made it out of my head and onto paper.

Acknowledgements

Five years ago or so during a conversation about financial matters, my friend Sylvia Lafferty said, "I know I should learn about money, but unless it's in a novel, I'll never get it." Thank you, Sylvia, for the idea for this book.

Thank you, Kerrie Droban – for being the first reader of every chapter, for teaching me so much about writing, for all of your helpful suggestions, for being such an amazing role model as a writer.

To my editors, Jean Krygelski and Carol Webb, and proofer, Bill Simpson, thank you for your keen eyes for details.

Many thanks to Andrea Witte for the book's title.

For a most awesome book cover, thank you Tanya Gagnon, and to illustrator, Marc Collins, thank you for doing such an incredible job of capturing the essence of my characters in art.

To article contributor, Angelika Reiss, and content critiquers, Keith Cuvelier, Mark Hughes, Lauri Rogers, and Sean Murray, thank you for sharing your expertise with my readers.

To intellectual property attorney, Connie Mableson, and patent attorney, Sandra Etherton, thank you for your patience in answering all my questions about copyrights, patents, and contracts over the course of this project.

And especially for my mom, a woman ahead of her time and my first financial teacher, thank you for showing me the value of being an entrepreneur before I could spell it.

One

Less than a week ago Rita Sterling and her husband Cliff were clinking wine glasses over steaks on the patio. Now she was grieving over his casket.

"What's wrong?" She had found him in the bedroom, frantically stroking his throat. When the response was desperate eyes and beads of perspiration, she ran to the phone. While she responded to the 911 operator's questions and listened to assurances, Rita convinced herself it was heartburn. He was a slender, healthy-looking, 52-year-old CEO of his own technology company. *Indigestion*.

By the time it took her to finish the insurance paperwork, Cliff had been covered with sticky monitor patches strung to machines, and hooked up to multiple IV drips. When he saw her approach, he mouthed, "I love you," then closed his eyes. Aside from the bluish tint from the fluorescent lighting, she thought he looked pretty good. She kissed his cheek and stepped just outside his treatment room to thank the paramedics. Out of the corner of her eye she saw Cliff's body jerk violently. As she rushed to his side, he grabbed a fistful of flesh on his chest and attempted to take a breath. The machines alarmed, and "code blue" sounded over the loudspeakers. Their eyes locked, and they spoke silently for a few seconds before medical personnel squeezed her away. Tears gushed while she watched the crowd perform in desperate, orchestrated chaos. She already knew what the doctors would concede. In their wordless conversation the couple had said their goodbyes.

~

Rita woke with a start, jolted as though someone had poked her with an electric shock. For a few seconds she was disoriented. She was on the floor of their closet with one of Cliff's suit jackets draped over her and a pair of his jeans rolled up for a pillow. Then it came back to her. Last night she had gone into the walk-in closet to throw her clothes in the hamper when her nose caught a whiff of Cliff's cologne. Her attention had been drawn to the suit he'd been wearing the day they met. She pushed the other suits aside to look at that one, then closed her eyes and allowed herself to recall every detail. His company, SterTechCo, was launching some sort of cutting edge software, and she was sent to interview him for a local news station. She was beyond nervous. This was not only her first assignment as a reporter, but she didn't know anything about technology, and her degree was in liberal arts, not journalism. She arrived in the reception area of his office with words swirling in her head, words she struggled to pull together into questions. When Cliff approached her and extended his hand to introduce himself, all her fears dissipated. He was dressed in a navy pin-striped suit over a crisp white button-down shirt with a polka-dot tie, and had a smile that took her breath away. His confidence and friendly manner were mesmerizing. Before she knew it, the interview was over, and she couldn't remember a single thing either one of them had said. The following morning he called the station and asked her out.

The gurgle of the coffeemaker in the kitchen drew her back to the present. Not yet. She wasn't ready. Tears began to swell. Damn it. This wasn't fair. He was too young. Fifteen years together had been too short. Rita buried her face into Cliff's lapel and sobbed.

The sound of dishes – someone was in the kitchen. She pulled herself off the floor, rubbed the crusted tears from her eyes, and headed toward the noise.

Rita pushed open the swinging door and found her stepson. Brian stood at the counter, dressed in the shirt and pants he had worn at his dad's service the day before, and spooned chunks of fruit from a large serving bowl onto a salad plate. A curl of his sandy-colored hair hung in the middle of his forehead, and his facial stubble glistened in the light coming from the window over the sink.

"I'm sorry. Did I wake you?" he asked.

"I'm not sure you could call it sleeping. I think I just went through the motion." Rita pulled out a chair, sat down and began to rake her fingers through her very red hair.

"Can I get you something? There's plenty of food leftover from yesterday," Brian offered.

"Just coffee would be fine."

Brian pulled two mugs from the cabinet, filled one for Rita and handed it to her before returning to the counter. He carefully sealed the Saran wrap around the bowl, put it in the refrigerator and joined Rita with a cup of coffee and plate of fruit. "Thanks for letting me crash in the guest house last night. I always feel close to Dad when I'm there."

"It seems like yesterday when you and your dad built that." Rita stirred in a splash of Coffee-Mate. "We had just gotten married. You were what, a senior in high school?"

"Yeah, and I was pretty messed up back then. Mom had died at the beginning of my junior year, and I still missed her a lot. I was on the fast track to nowhere when Dad came up with the idea to build the guest house. He said it was in case Grandma came to live with us, but I knew it was about me. Probably wouldn't be in line for partner at my accounting firm if it hadn't been for that project."

"We were concerned about the choices you were making and the friends you were keeping," Rita said. "He figured that if you were busy and tired, you'd have less time to get into trouble."

"Of course he was right." Brian walked to the coffee pot, poured himself another cup and stared out the window at the mission-style bungalow, nestled in the corner of backyard just left of the pool. It blended into the landscape as though it had always been there. A canopy of mature mesquites had grown to shade the whole structure. A bougainvillea adorned with bright pink flowers hugged the doorway. Clay pots in front supported a host of spring flowers.

Rita interrupted his thoughts. "I remember the day you finished the house, just a week before you were to start at Pima College. The three of us walked through every room while you two patted each other on the back for the great job you did." She smiled and swiped a tear from her cheek. "Then we stopped in the middle of the living room. He turned to you and asked, 'So, what do you think of your new place?' If you could have seen the look on your face."

Brian blinked back a tear. "God, I'm going to miss him."

Rita walked over, put her arm around him and rested her head on his shoulder. Moments ticked by while the warmth of the morning sun streamed through the window.

Brian thought aloud. "Maybe if I had stayed longer, been able to take some of the pressure off Dad, maybe he wouldn't have had a heart attack." His voice trailed off.

"It was time for you and your sister to go out on your own," Rita assured him. "And he knew that."

"Differences of opinion," Brian said. "That's what it boiled down to. We had different ways of looking at things. Maybe I should have kept my mouth shut, let him run the company his way and do what he wanted me to."

"He didn't raise you or Christine that way. And I don't think staying would have changed anything."

Soothing Brian's second guesses was easier than easing hers. Rita had concerns over the last few months, which Cliff quickly and consistently dismissed – a tingling in his arm, too much time at the computer, discomfort in his chest, heartburn, his restless sleep, not enough time in the day, a diet devoid of healthy choices. Maybe if she had pushed harder toward a check up, prepared more meals at home, maybe ... .

Brian interrupted her thoughts. "I better get going. I promised Jade I'd plaster the new wall she put up between the dining room and kitchen."

"Jade? I didn't know you knew her that well." Rita tried to remember the last time they had even been in the same room together. Her best guess – many Christmases ago, give or take.

He shifted his weight. "Oh, we don't really. We found ourselves in the same corner at the service yesterday, and we got to talking about the major remodel she was doing at her house and what Dad and I did with the guest house. It's no big deal. It's just skimming some drywall mud."

"Well, that is very nice of you," Rita said.

"That's me, the nice guy." He grinned. "So we're meeting at Larry's office at two o'clock to go over Dad's will, right?"

"Yes, but are you sure you want to go over to Jade's today?"

"I think the physical work will be good for me, and I still have a few more days before I go back to the office," he said, placing his coffee cup in the dishwasher. "Is there anything I can do for you before I take off?"

"No, no, you go. I'm fine." Rita struggled to put on a brave face. "I've got some things to take care of around here. I'll see you later."

"I can pick you up, if you'd like."

"Actually, your sister offered."

"Okay, then. I'll see you this afternoon." He gave her a peck on the cheek, headed out the back door toward the guest house and bumped into the pool service technician in the process.

Watching Ken check the pool's chemicals, Rita realized suddenly – *she* was now responsible for taking care of *everything*.

What did it cost for pool service, utilities? What were the mortgage payment and car payments? Did they have any savings? Investments? Did he make any arrangements to replace his salary? Life insurance? Surely his company was worth something. Her salary had always been just wardrobe money. Cliff paid for everything else. Questions and worries made her dizzy.

Rita grabbed the counter and steadied herself. A deep breath. No need to worry. That afternoon she'd learn the answers. Cliff had taken care of everything. Or had he?

---

*Go to the Appendix for the article entitled **What to Do When Your Spouse Dies** and for the **Estate Paperwork Tracking Table**.*

Two

Jade Hastings squinted at the hot morning sun streaming through the bedroom window. Too early to get up, too early for summer, she thought, as she lay still in the sweat-soaked sheets. Perspiration had matted her Irish red highlights into her otherwise brown hair and pasted the oversized T-shirt to her light brown skin. She squeezed her eyes shut. The heat caught Tucson's residents by surprise, which meant there hadn't been time to get the cooler in working order. Not that a forewarning would have changed anything for Jade. Long hours at the office had been consuming her life. Her house was a mess. She was exhausted and facing another day mired in the same predicament that Cliff complained to Rita about during the last couple of months of his life – overwhelmed, not enough time, lack of control. Was she far behind? All she had ever known was work, and it had cost her first marriage. Did she know how to have a relationship? Her parents were high school sweethearts and in love until the day her father died. Jade had not inherited the until-death-do-us-part gene.

She checked the time on the alarm clock and yawned. Half an hour before Brian was to come by. She peeled herself out of bed, pulled the damp T-shirt over her head, grabbed a robe from the knob on the headboard, and allowed her nose and ears to guide her toward the Columbian blend, dripping and hissing in the kitchen. Her semi-conscious state was interrupted when her toes collided with a group of paint cans just inside the kitchen. One fell over. She swore. Seconds ticked before her brain registered that all lids had been properly secured. She exhaled and continued toward the now silent pot of coffee. Maybe Brian could create a better staging area for construction materials besides the major thoroughfares.

The doorbell buzzed. Jade quickly glanced at the ears on the puppy wall clock. *He's early. Damn.* There was no time for a shower. She ran to the front of the house and yanked on the heavy door as Brian began to pick up his red Craftsman toolbox. The collision of the inside and outside air flipped the silk wrap away from her leg, which stopped Brian cold as he found himself eye level with the wind's mischief. She noticed his pause. His eyebrow arched a bit. He liked what he saw. And Jade liked what she saw. She hadn't been able to take her eyes off of him at Cliff's service. The last time she had seen Brian was when he was a young college freshmen at one of Rita's parties. The years had filtered out the immaturity and filled in some muscles. Whiplash good looking. Mental head slap. She'd been down the relationship road a few times, and she wasn't a very good driver, or passenger for that matter. As tempting as he was, now was not the time for another ride.

"Hi, Brian." The words snapped him out of his temporary trance and into motion.

"Sorry I'm early," he said, darting past her. "It wasn't as busy as I thought it would be at Lowe's."

Jade followed him into the kitchen. "No problem. Coffee's done, if you're interested."

"Maybe in a few minutes." He spoke to the wall as he popped the lid of the joint compound container and began to mix a batch of drywall mud.

Jade settled into one of the chairs in the breakfast nook behind Brian and wrapped her hands around her coffee cup. "I really appreciate you coming by today, but it could have waited."

He was engrossed in his work. With the trowel in his right hand

Brian scooped a lump of mud from the bucket and dumped the compound onto the empty trowel in his left. Like an artist working from his palette, he cut away several small portions of mud from the left tool with the right, and swept it over the taped sheetrock, stepping back occasionally to critique the pattern of the texture.

"Uh, no," Brian said to the wall. "I'm taking a couple of extra days off from work, and it's good to get out of my head for a change."

Clicks of the wall clock kept time with Brian's hypnotic rhythm. "My dad could lay some mean mud," Jade's whisper broke the silence. "I sure do miss him."

"Did he move?" Brian continued his work.

"No, passed away last summer," Jade said.

Brian turned to face her; his cheeks blushed. "Oh, I'm sorry."

"Thank you." Jade took a sip of coffee, allowing the awkwardness to settle. "He was just a couple of years older than Cliff, uh, your dad, and it was quite sudden. Brain aneurysm." She paused. "We always think we have more time."

"Yeah," Brian said, slipping into thought. His hand tilted, and the mud on the trowel began to slide. "Oops." He quickly leveled the tool and turned back to the wall. "So, your dad did this sort of work?"

"Actually he was a painter by trade," she said. "Then he learned the other trades and eventually got into rehabbing. Dad loved old buildings. When I was little, we would drive through downtown Tucson most Sundays, while he recited the history of this adobe or that mansion he had painted over the years. We'd meander through the opulent neighborhoods and mud adobe barrios. People doing yard work would wave at us. Sometimes we'd stop and chat a couple of minutes. Everybody knew my dad ... and trusted him. Eventually, people started telling him about properties before they went on the market."

"I bet he picked up some great deals that way," Brian said, turning around to face Jade.

"I think they may have started out that way," she said. "But once love took over the project, all logic and profit went out the window."

"Got emotionally attached, did he?"

"Over the top. There's nothing wrong with leading with your heart, but in real estate it's got to be backed with numbers."

"In business of any sort," Brian said, bending down and balancing the trowels on the lip of the bucket. He tossed his work gloves on the drop cloth and joined Jade at the kitchen table. "Sounds like our dads had something in common. Toward the end, the same thing happened to my dad at SterTechCo."

"Rita seemed to think that everything was going well over there."

"About the time Christine and I left, Dad had let his love of the company distort the hard reality of the financials."

"Is SterTechCo in trouble?"

"I've been out of the loop for the last few years, so I'm not sure what the current situation is. We're meeting with Dad's attorney this afternoon. I suppose we'll know more then."

"Any guesses who might take over as CEO?"

"Hard to say. A few people have been there since the beginning, but I'm not sure the company needs a CEO with a history, as much as it could use a fresh set of eyes, someone outside the company."

"So you wouldn't be interested in the position?"

"No, no." Brian shook his head and waved off the notion. "Christine might have been at one time. As Chief Technology Officer she was more involved in the day-to-day operations and would have been a logical choice. But we've both moved on with our professional lives." Brian looked past Jade at the recently mudded wall and then at his toolbox. "Say, I don't have anything else to do before the meeting this afternoon if there's something else you'd like me to work on."

Jade checked the time, ran her appointment book and to-do list through her memory, and chewed on her lip. "Are you sure? I've got to get to the office shortly, and it doesn't feel right just leaving you in this mess." Paint-splattered drop cloths blanketed the entire floor, tools were mixed with pieces of lumber and boxes of tile, and piles of materials huddled next to walls. And the kitchen was only the tip of the construction chaos. Jade used the shotgun approach to home remodeling – each room bore the scars of initial demolition and little evidence of forward progress. Even the act of prioritizing the projects made her head spin.

"I'm sure. What do you want me to do?"

"Between the two of us we can move the new sink cabinet to the guest bath," Jade said as she screeched her chair away from the table and picked up the dishes. "Then, if you could set the new toilet and hook up the plumbing for everything, I will owe you big time."

"No problem." Brian rose from his chair and picked up his work gloves.

"Let me change clothes real quick, and I'll meet you in the garage." He nodded and headed for the back door. Jade took off toward the master bedroom.

She shut the door, threw her robe on the bed and headed for the laundry basket of work shirts and Levis. Hastily, she plucked out one of each, slipped them on, and ran a brush through her hair. She was excited … and grateful for the help. She missed doing things with someone, like her father … or a partner.

Jade picked up a hairbrush, then stopped in mid-stroke. She had buried herself in mind-numbing projects to fill the void of her father's death. She hadn't been ready to say goodbye to her father. He wasn't old. He had no warning. He didn't know that cardio-vascular conditions ran in his family.

Now Cliff. Two people in her immediate circle were gone – people with calendars, goals, email, and families who loved them; people living their lives like there was all the time in the world.

What did she want? She had no need to ask this question in earlier years; now in middle-age she could not avoid it. Becoming a partner for the architectural firm was *not* what she wanted. Lately, the position looked more beneficial for the company and less fulfilling to her. Yes, the salary was good and the position secure, she argued to herself, with words coded into her employment DNA by her father. Now it wasn't enough – and unfortunately, she had not been very good with money. She spent what she earned, which meant $432 in a savings account and no entrepreneurial slush fund that would enable her to leave her present position, which left her feeling trapped professionally. Then there was the longing to share her life and dreams. Her first marriage was over before the wedding dress got back from the cleaners and was still painful after nearly two years.

"Are you okay in there?" Brian yelled down the hall. Jade snapped back to the present.

"Yeah, yeah, sorry. I'll be right there." A glance at the alarm clock on the nightstand put her into rush speed. If she didn't hustle, she was going to be late for the Bruggeman presentation.

Three

Rita and Christine milled around the reception area of Larry's law firm. Décor was legal bland – off-white walls, hard-cushioned mahogany chairs with legs scuffed around the edges, wall art that could have just as well been hanging in a local hotel room, a few business magazines stacked on the small end table angled in the corner, the smell of paper recycled through the vents. The tall ceiling created an echo chamber, so voices were kept to whispers in the event of incoming calls. Somewhere along Rita's third lap pacing around the room, she heard her name from behind and braced herself. Getting a hug from Larry was like getting greeted by an overzealous Labrador Retriever. She turned around to find him bounding toward her with arms extended. There was the usual impact – brief and balance-defying – followed by an approval-seeking grin.

"From the looks of you, Christine must have been driving," Larry said.

"She gets her lead foot from her father," Rita responded.

"I offered to pick you up," Brian interjected as he approached the group.

Christine took a breath and crinkled her nose. "Yew. Couldn't you have cleaned up a little?"

"I didn't have a chance to take a shower after working at Jade's. Besides, I still love grossing you out, sis." He chuckled and attempted to give her a hug. Christine pushed him away and turned her head, flicking her long blonde hair in his direction.

"Let's get started," Larry interrupted in his legal voice and motioned toward the conference room.

Everybody selected one of the faux-leather armchairs which hugged the edge of the oval-shaped, walnut-veneered table in the center of the room, and settled in while Larry straightened the stack of papers in front of him. Without so much as a glance at them, he began. "Cliff was as straightforward as they come, so it should come as no surprise that his wishes were, too. Rita, Cliff bequeathed to you the house, all personal property, his retirement account, and $50,000 in life insurance proceeds. Brian and Christine, you each get $25,000 in insurance proceeds. He also bequeathed his 60% of SterTechCo stock equally to the three of you. As you may know, the rest of the shares are held by employees and a couple of investors who came in when Cliff started the company."

The three beneficiaries exchanged glances, surprised and confused. His controlling interest to the three of them? The kids had left the company, and Rita was an outsider. It made no sense.

Larry let the words sink in. Rita was the first to speak. "I didn't have anything to do with the business. Why include me?"

"This will was written when you two first got married. It was like a secret wedding present. He hoped that you'd eventually become involved in the company. If that didn't happen, he figured that SterTechCo would either go public or get bought up by a larger company. In either case he thought your share would be worth a lot of money someday."

He had been so worried lately, Rita thought. Something was wrong. A knot began to form in the pit of her stomach. She was afraid that "someday" had not yet come.

"Is there an inheritance tax?" Brian asked.

"In most cases beneficiaries do not pay tax on money they inherit, but depending on the size of the estate, it's possible the estate could owe taxes."

"Will Dad's estate be subject to taxes?" Brian continued.

"Probably not, but it'll take us a couple of months to compile the final accounting. That entails adding up the value of all the assets that your father owned sole and separate, as well as his portion of jointly-owned property. We will include personal property, cash, investments, insurance policies owned by him and, in this case, the value of his company. Then we will deduct liabilities against the estate such as the mortgage, car loans, credit card balances, and certain administrative costs and funeral expenses. We further subtract what is given to Rita as surviving spouse. The tax is calculated after taking into account what is called an *exclusion*."

Rita sat motionless. The knot tightened. Sole and separate, joint, assets, liabilities, investments, loans. She realized she knew absolutely nothing about their financial lives. He was older, he had been married before, and he was a successful businessman. She realized she had slipped into his financial life, and now he was gone without the two of them ever creating one of their own.

Larry went on. "As executor, I've requested a couple of business appraisals since SterTechCo was Cliff's largest asset, and I contacted Ned Cassaway as the company's CPA to put together current financial statements. In fact, I asked him to join us today to give you an update. Before I bring him in though, there's one more point I'd like to make. I'm sure you can appreciate the importance of a smooth transition for SterTechCo employees and clients. So the sooner you could decide on the new board of directors, the better. Agreed?"

"Agreed," Christine piped up. Brian nodded.

"Excuse me." Rita raised her index finger, and all eyes looked at her. "This is all happening so fast, and I'm feeling overwhelmed. I'm still trying to come to terms with losing my husband, and now we've got to pick a new board right away? Can't that wait?"

Larry shook his head. "A company can't last long without leadership. SterTechCo is no different."

"I've never been involved in SterTechCo, or any company for that matter," Rita said. "How do I decide who should sit on the board?"

"The key employees at SterTechCo are still the same as when Brian and Christine were there," Larry said. "I'm confident that amongst the three of you, you'll be able to assemble a new leadership team."

Rita looked across the table at Brian, then at Christine.

"Larry's right," Brian said. "We'll get together and figure it out. We have no choice." Christine shrugged, nodded and stewed. Her father never took her seriously as a member of the management team, and now he gave his *wife* part interest in the company … someone who doesn't know the difference between a PIN and a VPN. What was he thinking?

Rita was mired in her own internal dialogue. "Too much, too much," she wanted to scream. She didn't want to make a decision about board members. She wanted to miss her husband and just curl up on the couch. She wanted to leave her big girl pants neatly tucked away in the dresser drawer. She wasn't ready; she didn't want to be ready. Why didn't Cliff prepare her? Why didn't she learn more? Why didn't she get her head out of her world and more into his?

"I'll draw up the necessary paperwork after you've made your choices." Larry's voice broke her train of thought. "Can I ask Ned to join us?"

The trio nodded in unison, and Larry shot out the door. A few minutes later Ned lumbered in carrying an accordion-style briefcase tucked under his arm. His lightweight suit was creased in all the wrong places from hours of sitting at a desk, and his shirt and tie strained to stay in place. Ned flopped in one chair and situated the leather case onto the chair next to him. He took a deep breath and dabbed the sweat from his forehead with a handkerchief. "I'm sorry I couldn't make it to the service yesterday. With April 15th just around the corner, it's crazy at the office. I'd known Cliff a long time. He was a great guy."

"Thank you, Ned, we appreciate that," Rita spoke for the group.

He nodded. After a brief dig through the briefcase's darkness, he produced a stack of papers and began distributing them among the table's participants like he was dealing from a deck of cards. "The first report is a Cash Flow Statement showing income and expenses. The first column reflects year-to-date numbers; the second, last fiscal year. I want to draw your attention to the last line, which shows a negative number in each column. SterTechCo has been operating in the red for over a year." All eyes at the table followed along with the stapled sheets in front of them. "If you'll turn to the next page, which is the Net Worth Statement, and notice the bottom line, you'll see a positive number. Primarily that's due to cash reserves, which Cliff put away after completion of the Tucson Medical Center job year before last." He took a breath. "The bottom line is that at its present level of expenses and without a significant infusion of cash, the company has about two months before it runs out of money."

Two months? Out of money? Rita couldn't believe her ears! How could that be?

"I know SterTechCo hasn't had a big contract in a while," Christine began, "but I thought that at least the maintenance contracts were keeping the doors open."

"If you look at the line entry for those contracts on the Income Statement, I mean the Cash Flow Statement, without that income SterTechCo would have been out of business months ago," Ned explained.

Brian spoke up. "Dad must have known what was happening. What was he doing about it besides bidding on new contracts?"

"He took a pay cut, borrowed, and liquidated personally." Ned shook his head. "I watched your dad grow this company into a leader in its field, but lately, with other companies getting the contracts, he was frustrated as hell."

Christine straightened her back along with the papers in front of her. "Thank you for putting this information together for us today. You've given us a lot to think and talk about." Eyes darted around the room, and everybody shifted. "We'll give you a call if we have any questions."

Ned nodded and gathered his belongings. "Yes, of course," he said as he left the room.

"There must be some mistake," Rita said. "Am I the only one who's in shock?"

Brian and Christine looked at each other and then at Rita. "I hoped the news would be a little better," Christine answered, "but I'm not surprised with the state of the company."

"You knew what was going on? And you walked away? Leaving your father to carry this burden alone?" Rita asked in a strained tone.

"It wasn't like that," Brian said. "We tried, but we didn't share Dad's vision for the company. Since there was room for only one CEO and it was his company, Sis and I bowed out."

"I'm sure you could have worked something out," Rita said. "He was so proud of you kids."

"He had a fine way of showing it," Christine blurted, then swallowed hard. "I'm sorry. I didn't mean it to come out that way. I loved Dad, but he wasn't the easiest guy to work for."

"I see," Rita said.

Brian spoke up. "Rita, there's a lot for us to talk about, so when we wrap up here, we'll figure out a meeting time."

Rita's anxiety was rising. SterTechCo was in trouble, big trouble, and she feared the news she had just heard was only the tip of her financial worries. What else didn't she know?

Brian addressed Larry. "Is there anything else we need to do at this point?"

"Actually, Rita," he said, turning toward her. "I need for you to gather up all your personal financial statements – checking, savings and investment accounts, the mortgage company, car loans, credit cards – and drop them off with Kathy, my assistant, as soon as possible."

"Cliff kept all important papers in the den. I'll see what I can find."

Larry made eye contact with each family member. "Well, if there's nothing else, I guess that does it for today." In silence Rita tucked the papers into her purse and rose from her chair while Christine and Brian pushed away from the conference table and rolled their stacks into tubes. Larry escorted the group to the reception area where mumbled, run-together words of condolences and goodbyes filled the air until the Sterling family found themselves outside under a canopy of wispy clouds. For a few awkward moments they sucked in the fragrance of budding desert blooms and let the afternoon's information sink in.

"How about meeting for coffee tomorrow morning?" Christine suggested. "Let's say 10:00? Blue Willow?"

"Sure," came out in soft unison.

"I've got some errands to run. Brian, would you mind taking Rita home?"

"If she doesn't mind being seen in my less-than-pristine, not-yet-classic ride."

"Not at all," Rita agreed quickly. "It'll give my heart a chance to get back to its normal rhythm. Between the Indy 500 ride over here and the disturbing news, I could use some calm and quiet."

"I'll see you both tomorrow," Christine said, waving in a cloud of exhaust dust.

Brian and Rita shook their heads as they watched Christine's Porsche bathtub-model disappear, and silently made their way toward Brian's car. They allowed the radio's music to fill the void of conversation until they arrived at the house.

"I could help you go through Dad's papers if you want," Brian volunteered.

"Thank you," Rita said, "but I think this is something I need to face alone."

The sound of Rita's purse and house key landing on the entry table echoed in the foyer and resonated through the living room. Rita stood for a moment as her eyes swept the rooms. *Value of personal assets.* She had shopped her way to accumulating a lot of stuff, but she wondered if it was of any value. Rita took in a lung-filling breath and marched toward Cliff's den. Ready or not, she couldn't put off learning what was going on in the world she knew very little about.

Go to the Appendix for the article entitled **Willing to Transfer – Or Not** *for information on the use of wills, trusts, contracts and titling to transfer assets.*

Four

Lori Formor dropped her purse on the kitchen counter and listened. With six- and seven-year-olds the silence alarmed her. "Bob?"

"In here," he replied from the direction of their bedroom.

On her way down the hall she peeked in the girls' room. It was empty.

She opened their bedroom door. "I was worried for like a couple of seconds. Way too quiet around here. Where are Angela and Taunya?"

He stopped halfway through buttoning the shirt of his police uniform. The left side hung heavy with his career's badges and awards centered, spaced and stacked, according to protocol, above the shield. In uniform Bob was spit-and-polish from his military-style hair cut to the I-think-I-can-see-myself shine of his boots, which was why he was routinely chosen for recruitment posters and PR events. There wasn't a more *cop's cop* than Bob, a motor officer and a member of SWAT; and as a citizen there was no one you would rather have show up if you had an emergency.

"Next door, playing."

"Good," Lori said as she threw him on the bed and crawled on top. She tossed her red-framed eyeglasses on the nightstand and locked lips with him in a long, melt-all-the-metal-on-the-shirt kind of kiss.

When she finally let him up for air, he asked, "What did I do to deserve that, so I can remember to do it again?"

Nobody in her group of friends would have guessed that Rita would be the first to lose her husband, and certainly not twenty years this side of Social Security. Bob was the one with the dangerous profession, and there was an underlying collective concern for his safety. Lori had been a cop's wife for ten years and thought she had come to terms with the possibility of losing him, but Cliff's death made her wonder if she was even prepared financially for life without Bob – a sad realization for an experienced financial planner. She squeezed tighter. Her emotions had been all over the place since Cliff died. It was scary to think of life suddenly without Bob – alone, a single parent – and scarier yet, of life with Bob as his spending continued out of control. The truth was that for the moment she wanted to capture how it was when they first got married – before the girls, before their lives got so complicated, before money differences strained the fabric of their relationship. After Cliff's service, Lori had plowed through their financial papers, policies, and legal potpourri, and through the scenarios – without him, without her, without either of them. The hard reality was – they weren't prepared.

"Hello in there." Bob's voice broke Lori's mental sidebar.

"Oh, sorry. Ah, nothing in particular."

He checked his watch. "As much as I'd like to continue this discussion under the covers, I've got to get to work. Promise me that we'll pick up where we left off, say, when I get up tomorrow?"

"Deal. I also want to make time to talk about our finances," she bargained.

Gently rolling her off of him, he pushed himself to an upright position and continued dressing. "What's this all about?"

She swung her legs over the side of the bed. "I've come to terms with the danger that surrounds your job, but none of us know when our time is up. I could go, and honestly, you don't have a clue how I manage our money. I think it's time that you got more involved."

"Nothing's going to happen to you," he assured, buckling his Sam Brown belt and snapping the leather keepers into place.

"And it may not, but still I just want to talk."

"Okay, okay." He held up his hands in surrender. "Whatever you want to do in the afterglow I'm going to lay on you, fine by me." He winked, smiled, and drew her tightly against him until she felt the cold brass through her blouse. His lips lightly teased her neck. Tiny, hot bursts of air started at her ear and slowly continued toward her shoulder. Gently pushing the collar aside, Bob's lips began to outline the lace of her camisole.

A sound from the other end of the house turned the couple into mannequins. Breathlessly, they waited.

"Mommm!" sent them into motion.

"Sounds like we both have to go to work," he whispered.

Lori gave Bob an extra long hug before he disappeared out the front door and headed off toward work. Then she settled the girls at the kitchen table for homework time, before scavenging through the refrigerator for something that could be dinner. Cheese, tortillas, leftover chicken. Quesadillas. Perfect. Lori pulled the chicken from the bone into strips and shredded the block of cheese.

The talk with Bob wasn't going to be easy – it never was. She was a saver; Bob was a spender. And she was losing – big time. Over the years Bob had matched toy for toy with his co-workers, and with each new item came the same old argument. It was bad enough that the garage and side yard looked like a sporting goods boneyard, but the purchases were getting more frequent, expensive, and nonsensical. There were the designer clothes that the girls didn't need, the shotgun he bought for his 78-year-old father who could barely lift a bag of potatoes, and then there was the latest push for a new extended-bed, 4x4 crew-cab truck. Not that there was anything wrong with his old truck, but dealerships were making great deals. The price of gas had spiked, inventory was high, and from the thumbnail calculations the salesman did, the payments were affordable. Magic words to Bob's ears, a migraine for Lori.

The smell of burning tortillas brought Lori's attention back to the stove. A quick flip of the quesadilla revealed more black than brown. Phewy. She removed the pan from the flame, salvaged the non-burned side, reassembled the pieces, and brought the skillet back to the heat. Two minutes, flip, two minutes, cut and serve.

"Come on, girls. Let's clean off the table. Dinner's almost ready." The words set Angela and Taunya into motion. School books, pencils and paper were replaced by the golden brown pizza-cut quesadillas. Lori grabbed handfuls of salad from the premeasured bag of lettuce, made deposits in three small bowls, pulled a bottle of ranch dressing and jug of milk from the frig, and set everything on the table. The girls snatched paper napkins from the holder and forks from the drawer, and it was dinner.

The kitchen nook buzzed with girly giggles and the children's chatter about their day. Play, art projects, reading. Lori listened and smiled. This was what it was all about; this was what was important.

Lori's mind wandered back to their last big money talk about six months ago, shortly after a free weekend at a timeshare resort. She hadn't been wild about going in the first place, but several of Bob's co-workers had purchased units, and he was excited about trading weeks for condos around the world. The ride home had been tense – she said absolutely nothing, Bob parroted the host's sales pitch – but by the time they closed the garage door, she believed her husband understood their financial situation enough to forego any major purchases in the foreseeable future.

Several days later Bob showed up with a new motorcycle. Just like that. His rationale was extensive – going on weekend trips with the squad, saving on gas for the daily commute, reducing stress. She was so angry that he had made such a big decision without her; she was at a loss for words. She put her foot down – the bike had to go. He put his foot down – the bike was staying. The bike stayed ... and had been collecting dust for the better part of the last six months. When she had tried to control him, he pushed back, and all that was left was to make the monthly payments for the next four years, an addition to the other bills they didn't need. Their monthly income was being eaten up at piranha-speed, and it was all Lori could do to keep obligations current. More time spent marketing and networking to bring in new financial planning clients meant less time at home and at the girls' activities. She was growing more tired of working harder and more resentful of Bob's continued selfish, immature attitude toward their family's finances.

The celebrity psychologist on television caught Lori's attention. She squinted at the screen in the family room and strained to hear what he was saying. The caption, along the bottom of the screen in bright yellow, described the scenario – *Couple at odds over each other's spending habits.*

"Often times money problems don't have anything to do with money," the therapist said. "What I mean is that sometimes there's something else going on, a deeper problem that is being masked by financial irresponsibility. And that's what it is, isn't it? We saw in the tape that you've got clothes in your closet with the tags still on them. So you agree that you don't need all those things you buy, right?" The guest nodded her head. "And you said that you've hidden purchases from your husband, right? Under the bed?" Another nod. A laugh from the audience. "Well, I guess your hiding days are over now, huh?" the therapist joked.

"Can we have Skinny Cows for dessert, Mommy?" Angela's question snapped Lori's attention away from the screen.

"Yes, you may," Lori replied as she walked to the freezer. She pried open the plastic container; the girls helped themselves to a frozen dessert from the tray and ran toward the family room.

Lori watched Taunya switch the remote to the Disney channel, then sit on the floor next to her sister in front of the television. She stacked the plates, gathered the silverware, and began to load the dishwasher while her thoughts returned to the show. Was there something going on with Bob that she hadn't noticed? Something besides the usual silence surrounding his work? The truth was they hadn't talked about important things like dreams and goals since the girls were born. Too busy with life, too easy to put the days on automatic pilot. Their situation didn't warrant a celeb intervention, but something had to give … and soon.

Five

Marla Cassaway flicked the light switch. Nothing. Great. Another item to add to the to-do list. Zane and Zach, her seven-year-old twins, pushed to get around her, but Marla stuck her arm out. "Whoa, you two. Let me get a light on. I don't want you to trip over something."

Her hands tapped the walls and counter until they found the switch for the light over the sink. The boys pushed past her as the fluorescent flicker exposed the stack of post-noted tax client files on the kitchen table.

Damn it. With all the time he spends at the office, why does he have to bring this clutter home? Marla silently reprimanded her husband Ned, then stopped. Maybe she was being too hard on him. At least she still had her husband. She couldn't imagine what her friend, Rita, was going through. She couldn't imagine what she would do without Ned.

They had met in college through a mutual friend and were married shortly after graduation. Parents on both sides were traditional, so Marla looked forward to being a wife and stay-at-home mom. Life and love had been comfortable during their twenty-year marriage. That was, until Cliff died. Since then, every night it was the same nightmare … she and the kids huddled together on a small island while they watched the water's edge lap closer and closer toward them. In ankle-deep water Marla told herself it was only a dream and commanded herself to wake up. She couldn't move. Panic. Loud heart beats. Silent scream. Finally, a violent jerk, and her eyes would open. She was alone … and responsible. What if something happened to Ned? Where would that leave her and the boys? How would she take care of them?

Marla's thoughts were interrupted by cries from the living room.

"Hey, no fair. I was playing with that," yelled Zane.

"Mom!" screeched his brother. "Zane isn't sharing!"

By the time Marla found the boys, they were on the floor in a tug-of-war over a dump truck, surrounded by enough toy vehicles to create a used car lot in their driveway.

"Alright. Let's put all these toys away and get you two in the bathtub," Marla said.

"But we're not done with our game yet," Zach pleaded.

"Maybe later. Your dad's going to be home soon, and I want you to be clean and fresh. Come on." The boys joined Marla in picking up everything off the floor and tossing handfuls into the storage box next to the couch. When the task was complete, the twins began to pull off their soccer uniforms, as they walked toward the bathroom, and let them drop to the tile. Marla followed, scooped up the discarded clothes, stuffed them in the hamper, and began running the bath water. Moments later Zane and Zach were on either side of Marla in bed, reading along in their favorite storybook, their eyelids getting heavier with each turn of the page. Halfway through page five, the boys were asleep. Marla eased off the mattress, picked up Zane and tucked him in, while Zach stirred slightly and dozed off.

Marla went to the hamper, retrieved the boys' uniforms and enough clothes for a load, and padded toward the laundry room. With the sound of water filling the washing machine, she headed for the kitchen. The blue tint of the fluorescent light did nothing but reveal the coldness of the room, much like the kitchen she grew up with. Sadly, her family's culinary lineage died two generations ago, leaving her to flounder in food-prep hell. If only Great Grandma Bennett was still alive, Marla wished. Trips to her house were few and early in Marla's life, but indelible. No matter the time of day or time of year, visitors were drawn toward the kitchen in a smell-induced trance – a pot of soup simmering on the stove, a freshly-baked apple pie, bread browning in the oven – to gather around the old drop-leaf with flour-filled cracks and vanilla stains. Marla glanced at her table overflowing with file folders, then to her three ovens, and sighed. Inspiration, that's what she needed. She grabbed the phone off the wall cradle and dialed.

"Hi, Sweetie. What's up?" her mother asked.

"I was just thinking about Grandma Bennett and wondered what ever happened to her kitchen table?"

"Why in the world would you want to know about that old thing?"

Marla could already hear her mother's sarcasm inching in on their conversation. She closed her eyes and took a deep breath. "I thought I could use some inspiration."

"Inspiration for what?"

"I thought I'd try making some of her recipes, and in a way it'd be like having her here."

Here it comes, Marla thought.

"You can watch cooking shows all day long and you're still not going to be a good cook," her mother insisted. "You just don't have the knack. I didn't either, and you kids didn't starve, right? Give the boys their daily chewables, and they'll be fine."

"It's not about vitamins, Mom," Marla said. "Or not having enough to eat."

"Just because you can't cook doesn't make you a bad mom."

"I know." The words were automatic, but not convincing. "Anyway, I'd really like to have Grandma's table if it's okay."

"Your Aunt Iva had it in her garage last time I heard. As far as I know, she's not using it. But it really doesn't go with your décor."

"Thanks, Mom. I'll give her a call. Talk to you later." Marla ended the call and cut off her mother's next curt comment.

A quick call to her aunt, and it was set for Marla to pick up the table the next day. Her excitement drove her to the cabinet where she stored the library of cookbooks she had purchased on impulse over the years. She gently retrieved a rubber-banded stack of handwritten recipes stained with their ingredients, seated herself at the table, cleared a small area, and began to read each slip of paper.

Headlights shone through the window. The car door slammed, and Marla rushed to the back door to greet Ned with a kiss. "How was your day, Honey?"

"Hectic, but the pile is dwindling," he said as he collapsed in a chair at the table, which groaned from the weight of its guest. "At the office at least," he finished, staring at the mess on the table. "I'll be glad when the 15th gets here."

"Can I get you anything to eat?"

"No, we ordered in at the office. Are the boys asleep?"

"They hardly made it through the bath. Soccer really wore them out today," Marla answered as she pulled out a chair next to her husband.

"What's all this?" he asked, picking up a piece of paper.

"Grandma Bennett's recipes."

"Doing some spring cleaning?"

"Actually, I thought I'd give them a try," she said with a shrug.

"What brought this on?"

"I've been doing a lot of thinking since Cliff's funeral … about family, about how I could be a better mom and better partner, how I could improve myself. You know it's always bothered me that I don't cook. I loved the feeling of Grandma's kitchen, so I made a commitment to learn how to really cook, and I figured what better place to start than with her recipes."

"You won't get any objections from me," Ned said and smiled. "I'm happy to be your guinea pig."

"I'm even going to get her old table."

"That's great." The words leaked out in a yawn.

Marla inhaled deeply. "I've also been thinking that I really don't know much about our finances."

"What's there to know?" The defensive tone took her by surprise.

"I don't know what I don't know. But I think I'd like to find out about money, our money," she answered.

His face flushed. "Money comes in; money goes out. Not much to it."

"This is important to me, Ned. I'd like to work on our finances together."

"Well, well … ." Her husband wasn't in the habit of stuttering. "I suppose that would be okay."

"Good. How about this weekend?"

By the time a strained "alright" escaped from his lips, Marla had given herself a mental high-five and was well on her way to giddiness about these new activities. "I was also thinking about taking an investment class. What do you think?"

"Oh, fine … listen, I'm going to work on these in my den for a while," he said, gathering the stacks of bulging manila folders and his briefcase. She turned around in time to catch a breeze and the door closing.

~

In almost one continuous movement, Ned deposited the armload of files in the recliner and made his way behind the desk. *Great. This is all I need with tax returns due in a few weeks.*

He dropped into the worn leather chair and pulled the stack of semi-monthly bills from the briefcase. After setting aside the utility statements, he grabbed the credit card statements he had received in the morning's office mail. His eyes grew wider as he began to read the list of vendors and the charges. A bead of perspiration punctuated each line; each statement ratcheted up the panic. He flipped back to the first page of each statement, gulped at the total due, and took a deep breath at the minimum.

Ned's fingers flew across the desktop calculator as he thumbed through the stack of statements and compared that total with the checkbook balance. He heaved a sigh. The extra work from tax season had kicked up his take home enough to cover everything with a few dollars to spare.

His heart thumped hard and deep in his chest. What was there to be relieved about? This weekend Marla was going to find out what he had done.

Six

Bob and Lori lay next to each other in perspiration-soaked sheets and stared at the ceiling. A quickie in the afternoon, between the close of the stock market and their girls' arrival home from school, was the only sliver of intimacy for them since Angela and Taunya were born.

"Oh, baby, that was good," Bob said, still breathless after the afternoon's activity.

Lori rolled over, faced her husband and smiled. *Yes, that was good,* she thought. But then again, sex was always good. Money? Now that was a different story.

Bob looked over. "Whatcha thinking?"

"Oh, how it's been a long time since we really talked about … us, our future, our goals and dreams."

He rolled over onto his side and propped himself on his elbow so he was facing his wife. "Babe, I'm just trying to get to retirement."

The words were similar to many of Lori's clients who missed a lot of life while waiting for the retirement fairy to wave her magic wand and make their lives perfect. There were no guarantees, and Lori had been feeling frustrated lately watching their lives fly by on automatic pilot. "I know, but there's more to life than that," Lori said. "And there's a lot of life between now and then."

"Well, sure, but we're doing all right."

"Actually no, we're not."

He frowned, and his chin retracted a bit. "What do you mean?"

Lori took a deep breath. "At times I feel like we're not on the same page."

His face softened. "Didn't we just spend 30 minutes on the same page?" He winked. Lori blushed. "Glad to see I can still do that to you."

"Come on. Let's get serious for a minute."

"Oh, okay." Bob pulled the top sheet across his chest, slipped it under his arm and struck his "I'm listening" pose.

"Sometimes I feel like we're leading separate lives … kids and work pulling us in different directions. Remember how we used to have talks about our future together?" Lori asked.

"Yeah, I remember." He grinned. "We had to sit on opposite ends of the couch. Otherwise, we wouldn't get any talking done. Anyway, that was back when we were just starting out. The girls came along, and our future has been about raising them."

"That's just it. We're responsible for them and for ourselves. And I don't think we're doing a very good job on either count."

"We're responsible. We pay our bills."

"There's more to being responsible than paying the bills."

Bob rolled onto his back and stared at the ceiling fan's blades whirling the room's air. "This is about my spending, isn't it? You're saying I'm not responsible."

Yes, it's about your spending and yes, you are irresponsible, Lori wanted to scream; however, taking an accusatory stance would grind the conversation to a halt, and she had to keep the dialogue moving. The clock was ticking on their family's financial future, and she had to make him understand. "I'm saying we're not paying enough attention to what we're doing today that's impacting our future. This isn't about *my* spending or *your* spending. It's about *our* financial situation."

He turned to look at her. "You're the financial planner in the family. I thought you were taking care of everything."

"I'm a financial planner, not a miracle worker. All I'm doing is writing checks. Everything that comes in, goes out. That's what's been bothering me lately. If one of us wasn't bringing in a paycheck, we would be in a negative situation."

"Don't we have anything in savings?" There was an accusatory tone in his voice.

"Whatever I can put away only stays there until the next got-to-have item comes along."

"We work hard, and I like being able to buy what I want," Bob defended himself as he crossed his arms over his chest and went back to watching the ceiling fan. Of course he does, Lori thought. He does whatever he wants and leaves it up to me to figure out how we're going to pay for it.

"We're working hard to buy stuff," Lori said, "The more stuff we buy, the harder we have to work to pay for it. This is crazy, and we can't go on like this."

"What's that supposed to mean?"

"We're just treading water, barely keeping up with the monthly bills. We can't afford our lives. I'm exhausted. We need to make some changes."

"I talk with the guys at work, and it sounds like everybody's situation is pretty much the same," Bob said. "We work, we buy; we work to buy another day. Isn't that the American way?"

Everybody's situation is *not* the same, Lori thought. There's locker room talk, and then there's the real truth. Outward appearances can be very deceiving.

Lori injected her business voice. "Yes, and because it *is* the American way, most people, including us, are teetering on the edge of a financial cliff. Without changes now, we're going to end up where we don't want to be."

"Aren't you overreacting?" Bob cooed. "It can't be that bad."

"How would you know?" Lori snapped and sat up, drawing the sheet close to her body. "You have no idea what our financial situation is. You spend as though we have an endless source of money. We have to start making financial decisions together, and we've got to do some planning."

He shrugged and stroked her arm. "You're right, I don't know the particulars, but it seems to me that everything is going okay."

Lori shook her head and made eye contact. "Everything is not okay. We have to be a team. Otherwise, it won't work. This is not negotiable, Bob." She allowed the words to settle in before she continued. "So, when can we pencil in some financial date nights?"

A twinkle appeared in his eyes, and a grin began to form. "How about we work on the date part first?" Bob hooked his finger on the rim of Lori's sheet and slowly lowered it away from her body.

Typical response, Lori thought. Change from serious to sex.

"Not so fast," Lori said, pulling away. "I said *financial* date."

"Okay. You name it, and I'll be there."

The ring from the phone pierced the moment. "Don't answer it, babe," he whispered. "We've got some more time."

"It could be the kids," she said as she reached across him.

~

Rita opened the door to Cliff's den and stared at the massive walnut desk that had belonged to Cliff's grandfather, a cobbler, who had used it as much as a workbench since he had a desk. As long as her husband was alive, there was no talk of refinishing or restoring the piece of furniture; now that he was gone, she couldn't think of changing one nick, stain or drill hole.

She walked behind the desk and slowly sank into the vintage leather chair. Generations of sitting had taken its toll on the once taut, supple material, making it more of a sinkhole than a seat. Using the armrests to pull herself out of the cavity, she struck a balanced pose on the edge of the seat.

The middle drawer contained two checkbooks. Familiarity drew her to the one she had used many times. As her eyes scanned the entries, the numbers clicked off like a silent adding machine making her head spin. By themselves they had little meaning; together they were staggering. Month after month his salary had been consumed. Now with his salary gone ... . She thought of the insurance proceeds. It wasn't much; it wouldn't be enough.

The other checkbook was from a brokerage firm. Probably connected with an investment account, she thought. Not that she knew any of the specifics, but Cliff had mentioned his broker many times. The large numbers scared her. Big in, big out – deposits from unknown sources, checks to SterTechCo, transfers to their personal account.

She opened the bottom right drawer and removed the files – brokerage statements, confirmation receipts for stock purchases and sales. Rita wasn't sure what they had to do with her financial situation; however, the sheer volume put a knot in her stomach. With plenty of time she could figure out what they meant, but she needed answers fast. She checked the desk clock. Four o'clock. She picked up the portable phone from its cradle on the desk and punched in the number she knew by heart.

"Hi, Lori, it's Rita. I hope I'm not interrupting anything."

"No, not at all," her friend quickly replied. What's up?"

"Well, Larry wanted me to put together our financial records as part of settling the estate," Rita explained. "So I started going through Cliff's desk. The more I find, the more confused I get. You know, I'm not good at this."

"Would you like for me to look things over?" Lori asked.

"Would you? Larry wanted me to turn everything over to him, but I'd really like your opinion."

"My schedule is pretty open the next couple of days."

"I'm meeting Brian and Christine at Blue Willow at ten. Could we get together there at 9:30?"

"Sure."

"Thanks, Lori. I really appreciate it."

"That's what friends are for. I'll see you then." They clicked off.

Rita was relieved. Professional help was hours away. Her friend would figure everything out. Rita assured herself that she was probably missing something that would settle the financial turmoil she had found. She took another deep breath and opened the next drawer which contained pages of credit card statements. Cliff had always encouraged her to use cards. Made it easier to write just one check, he would say. He never commented on how much she charged or what she bought. He just loved her. But there were so many entries, so many charges that she couldn't remember. It seemed ridiculous now.

Another drawer appeared to be the current bill depository. Rita retrieved a calculator from the middle drawer, added the amounts in the stack of monthly obligations, and compared the calculator's digital display with the ending balance in the checkbook. There was an audible sigh of relief when she realized there was enough – barely – at least for the time being. She had the salary coming in from her job as a news reporter, but without the insurance money soon, she wasn't sure how she was going to make next month's bills.

After cleaning out the desk and placing its financial contents into the awaiting file box, Rita allowed herself to sink into the chair's comfortable leather. Her gaze fell upon a picture of her and Cliff on the beach in La Jolla. "If I didn't love you so much, I'd be pretty pissed at you right now," she whispered, turning her wedding band. "Why didn't you tell me what was going on? I was your wife. I had a right to know."

Frustrated, she exhaled, reached for the cardboard lid, and shimmied it into place just in time for it to catch a teardrop. Staring at the wet spot, Rita proclaimed, "That's enough of that." As she hoisted the box from the floor, her glance fell upon the picture again. "I'm not sure what you got me into, but I have a feeling I don't have much time to figure it out."

Seven

Blue Willow's breakfast aromas suddenly rendered Rita famished. With her gaze on the dining room, she snaked her way past the obstacle course of card and novelty displays and slow moving shoppers, and found Lori seated in the mist-cooled, mesh-covered patio area, drinking ice tea and reading the Wall Street Journal.

"What do you have there?" Lori asked Rita as she approached.

She positioned the box between them. "My financial life. Or at least what's left of it."

The server refilled Lori's glass with red Zinger and handed Rita a menu. "I know what I want. Spinach and bacon omelet with potatoes and raisin toast. And the ice tea looks good."

"A little hungry, are we?" Lori folded the newspaper and set it aside.

"This place does that to me. Aren't you having anything?"

"No, as usual I finished the kids' breakfast."

"Thanks for meeting with me on such short notice."

"Don't give it a second thought. I'm happy to do whatever I can."

Rita drew a breath. "Larry wanted me to put together our personal financial information as part of settling the estate. At first I was just going to throw everything in a box and give it to his assistant, but my curiosity got the best of me, and I started looking at the statements. The more I read, the more concerned I got." The sensation hit again. "I'm afraid I'm in big financial trouble."

"What did you find?" Lori leaned forward.

"Maybe enough money to get me to the end of the month, and a lot of transfers between accounts. That's when I called you. I need to know my bottom line and fast."

They fell silent while their server positioned Rita's meal.

"What happened at Larry's office yesterday?"

Rita picked up a forkful of eggs, then let it rest on the edge of the plate. "Cliff left me $50,000. An insurance policy. I had no idea. Of course, all of our personal property. Oh, and 20% interest in Ster-TechCo, which according to Ned is only a few months away from closing its doors."

Lori sipped her tea and watched her friend manage a few bites of toast. "The insurance money gives you a few options, but I'll know more once I've gone through your box. Together we can talk about how things look – tomorrow if you'd like." She paused a moment. "Have you given any thought about where you want to go from here?"

"Not a lot. Short-term, I figured you'd work out all the financial stuff, invest my money to make up for Cliff's salary and give me a budget. That'd give me plenty of time to work on long-term because I'll be financially comfortable." Rita grinned.

Lori chuckled. "I'm glad you said that with a smile because without even looking at your box, I'd venture to say that the income from investing $50,000 is not going to replace Cliff's salary."

Rita pushed her mostly untouched breakfast away, and their server quickly made it disappear.

Lori continued. "We've never discussed the details of your finances, but generally, any loss of income will have an impact on the family budget. How much depends on other resources. Besides what you have here, can you think of any other assets, like a collection of something? Stamps? Coins?"

"I don't think so." Rita rolled the napkin on her lap and ran it through her fingers. "As far as I know, everything is in this box, but like

I said, Cliff handled all that. We lived well, and I wasn't interested in learning the details."

The face of the worried widow stared back at Lori, and it broke her heart. Without even popping the lid on the box, Lori had learned to recognize the signs of potential financial disaster. The main breadwinner dies. Little or no insurance proceeds or sufficient assets exist to make up for the loss of income. The financially oblivious surviving spouse is left to carry on. More than ever Lori wanted the outcome to be different for her friend than it had been for the widowed clients who had sought advice before her. If only wanting was good enough.

"I'll get busy, and then we could talk tomorrow. How does that sound?" Lori asked.

"Like a plan. I feel better already." Rita blew out a sigh and smiled.

"Looks like we finished just in time," Lori remarked as her eyes noticed Brian and Christine walking toward them. "I've got to run. What time works for you tomorrow?"

"Are you having lunch with Marla and Jade?" Rita asked.

"Yes, same time, same place. Do you want to come?" Lori answered.

"That's what I was thinking. Then, if you're available, you and I can talk over dessert."

"We can do that. I'll take care of this," Lori said to Rita as she snapped up the check off the table. "And this." She hoisted the file box from the floor. "See you tomorrow."

However, her turn to leave came to an abrupt halt when her cardboard cargo knocked Christine into her brother. "Sorry, obviously I haven't learned how to drive this thing yet," Lori said to the pair, glancing at the box. "Well, I'm late for a meeting. Nice seeing you two again. Bye, Rita," she said over her shoulder.

After fresh drinks were ordered, sipped, and to the group's satisfaction, Christine was the first to speak. "I'm afraid I don't have a lot of time this morning … technical crisis as I was leaving the office. Did you both get a chance to look at what Ned gave us yesterday?" When Rita and Brian nodded, Christine continued. "I don't know what you thought, but the bottom line looks pretty grim to me."

"I agree, and two months isn't much time," Brian said.

Rita had glanced over the pages of numbers she received at Larry's office before the search of Cliff's desk, but at this point she was on numeric overload and felt the financial walls beginning to close in. The sheer volume of money transfers on the personal side was alarming and reeked of panic. She needed to hear good news from Cliff's children, assurance that there was some way out of SterTechCo financial skids.

"That almost sounds like you're giving up without even trying." Rita attempted to stifle her frustration at their matter-of-fact attitude.

"Not giving up, just being realistic," Brian said.

"Are you saying SterTechCo can't be saved?" Rita asked.

Brian shrugged. "Hard to say. We saw signs that perhaps the company had run its course. Dad didn't, which is one of the reasons we left."

"But from what I could understand from your dad, everything was going well." Rita's voice cracked under the weight of the news.

Christine jumped in. "That was his reality. He was hanging on to what worked when he started the company, but today's technological environment demands flexibility, and unfortunately, Dad wasn't willing to listen to the voice of change."

"Are you proposing we just shut down the company?" Rita swallowed hard.

"Over the years several competitors have voiced an interest in acquiring SterTechCo. We could explore that option," Christine addressed them as fellow members of the board of directors.

Rita's head was swimming. This couldn't be happening. Two weeks ago everything was fine. Cliff was fine. They were happy; they lived comfortably. Now her dear husband, who had taken such good care of her, was gone. There were more bills than money to pay them. The company she thought was a thriving enterprise was on the verge of collapse, and his kids were talking about selling it.

"I can't believe that you're being so nonchalant about giving up on what had been your dad's life's work," Rita said.

"I know it sounds that way," Christine said in her daughter's voice. "But we tried to talk to Dad about this many times, especially leading up to both of us leaving last year. He wouldn't listen, and we couldn't watch any more."

There was so much she didn't know. Cliff had kept so many secrets. Rita kept her eyes on Christine. "Tell me what happened."

Christine grabbed her long blonde hair with both hands, formed a ponytail, then flipped it behind her. "SterTechCo is in the business of systems integration software – basically, getting different systems to be able to talk to one another. In the beginning the focus was in the medical field, and all work could be done in-house. Then Dad decided he wanted to expand to other areas like government agencies and larger projects, which meant that the company had to partner with outside vendors in order to meet contract requirements." Christine took a sip of tea, dumped another sugar packet into the glass, stirred, and continued. "He never really liked the partnering concept – viewed it as a necessary evil, a loss of control. After the first contract, the word was out that Dad was hard to work with, and the list of potential players dwindled, which made bidding on certain projects undoable. For the contracts we *were* awarded, the technical burden fell on SterTechCo employees who were always buried in the latest project-driven learning curve and pushed by unrealistic deadlines. I'd ask for more engineers, but Dad would always nix the idea. He didn't want to lay anybody off if we didn't get the next contract, so projects were always understaffed and over budget."

As Rita listened, she recalled conversations she and Cliff had over the years, and a lot started to make sense. For him it was about control – his company, his rules. Partnering, even when it involved his own children, was not easy for Cliff. When the kids had been with SterTechCo about a year, she broached the subject of awarding some stock to them. The suggestion was met with such strong opposition that she never brought it up again – something about irreconcilable professional differences. That's what made Cliff's will so curious. If he and the children had a falling out about the company's future, why did he leave it to them – and her? Did he have a change of heart? Or didn't he get around to updating the will?

Brian interrupted her mental sidebar. "When we weren't awarded a contract, Dad had the tendency to want to make up for lost revenue in the next bid." He shook his head. "The bids were so far out there that we didn't stand a chance of getting the projects. Eventually, Dad would hit a bull's-eye on a smaller deal, and we'd be afloat for a while. A few of us tried to talk to him about getting real with bid numbers, but he was the CEO and didn't want to hear it."

The server came by and topped off the tea glasses; the pause allowed the information to sink in for a couple of heartbeats. Maybe SterTechCo was on an unstoppable collision course, Rita feared. Had Cliff painted himself and his company into a professional corner where no one wanted to work with them? Was there still a place for them in the market? Did Cliff's dream of SterTechCo being a sustainable asset for Rita's future die with him? "Is it too late," Rita broke the silence, "to save the company?"

Brian drew a breath. "It would be tough. But maybe the better question is who's going to try? I'm on the partner track at my accounting firm."

Rita looked at Christine. She held up her hands. "Not me. My company's about ready to market a new software package."

"Is there someone at SterTechCo to take over?" Rita asked.

Christine chewed on her straw. "Of course, Dad's college buddy, Glen, is up there in the ranks as VP of sales, and, you know, has been there since the beginning. I'm not sure how he'd fly solo, though. Other than that, with a few exceptions the staff is a bunch of computer geeks. Speaking as their former leader, I can tell you that they're not much for climbing the corporate ladder."

"What about me?" Rita could have sworn that somebody else had spoken. The restaurant clatter seemed to hush while her heart thumped loudly in her throat.

Brian and Christine looked at Rita in speechless disbelief as though their dad had suddenly sat down beside them. "Nothing personal, Rita," Christine began slowly, "but you don't know the difference between a node and a knob. And what about the business side? You don't have any experience running a company."

"You're right," Rita said, "I don't have any knowledge of technology or any business experience ... but I care, I can learn, and I've got good people skills and problem-solving abilities." She wanted, no needed, this position. She feared that if SterTechCo went bankrupt, personal financial devastation wouldn't be far behind; she couldn't sit around the house and wait for it to happen. "I'm thinking of this as a joint venture. If you'd be willing to help in the planning and strategizing areas, Glen and I could handle the day-to-day operations."

Seconds ticked by before Brian broke the silence. "I agree with Sis, Rita. There's no disputing your intentions, but I'm not sure you know what you're letting yourself in for. The business is complicated. SterTech-Co's position in the world of technology is complicated. And I'm not sure Glen's going to be real keen on the idea of co-managing."

Rita straightened her back. "I don't know why, but for some reason your dad wanted me involved in the company, so I'm getting involved. I may not able to program or do accounting, but I'm willing to do whatever it takes to save SterTechCo. Let's see how it goes, and if the situation doesn't turn around fairly quickly, we could still solicit offers for purchase."

"Except that if we utilize all the assets to keep SterTechCo afloat and things *don't* pan out, then our acquisition potential would diminish," Christine said.

Rita opened her mouth, but Brian interrupted. "True, but you said it yourself, Sis. The financials look pretty grim. We could *succeed* and increase our net worth in the company."

Christine shrugged and nodded in agreement.

Brian leaned over the table. "If things don't work out, and the company doesn't look all that desirable for purchase, we will have given it our best shot, and it either happens or it doesn't. I don't think a couple of months are going to make a huge difference with potential buyers. In a nutshell, I think we've got more to gain than we've got to lose."

"Good points," Christine admitted, then turned her attention to Rita. "I think what you want to do is admirable, and just so you know up front, Brian and I have moved on with our professional lives. We can be a resource, but the majority of the responsibility for this undertaking is going to rest on your shoulders."

"I understand," Rita said.

"Good," Brian said. "How about the three of us meet with Saleem, Glen, Michelle and Kerry tomorrow morning to discuss the state of the company. After that, we can meet on an as-needed basis?"

The two women looked at each other. "Sounds good." Rita nodded.

"I'll set it up," Brian said.

Christine raised her glass. "I'm not convinced we have a prayer of pulling SterTechCo out of its downward spiral, but, what the heck, I'm always up for a ride."

Eight

Always the first to arrive, Marla thought, as she allowed herself to be seated at their usual table by the window. The restaurant had begun to fill, both with lunch patrons from the affluent foothills area, and the aroma of freshly baked bread. No sooner had she removed the napkin from her water glass, than a server presented a glazed saucer of seasoned dipping oil and a linen-enveloped loaf of crusted heaven. Marla had opened her mouth to wave off the temptation, but it was too late. The delectable duo had been placed within reach, and the server was already greeting the couple at the next table.

The battle with carb addiction began when Marla discovered better food through flour. The war raged on through years of yo-yo dieting in an effort to kick the habit and attain bodily perfection. Unfortunately, she hadn't been successful on either count. Then, after losing her waistline to the birth of her children, she wondered if she would ever meet her weight goals.

The current debate whether or not to eat the bread was listing toward surrender when she was rescued.

"Did you leave any bread for the rest of us?" Lori asked, cardboard box in tow.

"Thank you for getting here just in time. You're my hero," Marla said. "Is this a working lunch?"

Lori slid the carton under her chair and gave her friend a hug. "Rita wanted to go over some financial questions after lunch." She sat across from Marla and quickly tore off a piece of bread.

"Does that mean she's joining us today?"

Lori covered her mouth as she answered. "Yeah. I met with her briefly yesterday. How are you doing?"

"Ready to be done being a tax wife for a few months. I swear. Ned's been acting weirder than usual lately. Take last night. He got home late. I started to talk about getting more involved in our finances, and he got all defensive and protective like I was implying he hadn't been doing a good job."

"Is he?" Lori mumbled through a mouthful. "Doing a good job?"

Marla shrugged. "As far as I know. The utilities have never been turned off, and I haven't had a credit card swipe denied. I'm worried about him, I guess. He seems more stressed than ever. After what happened to Cliff, I'd like to take some pressure off of him. Besides, I think it's time I learn about money. How could I get started?"

"The choices are mind-boggling – the Internet, classes, books, CDs. It depends on what aspect of money you're interested in," Lori said.

"I'm not sure exactly, but I suppose I'd like to learn the basics."

"Sorry I'm late." In one swift maneuver Jade slung her purse on the back of the chair, sat down, and positioned a napkin on her lap. "Did I miss anything?"

"Marla's interested in learning about money."

"That sounds like fun. I must admit, I'm basically money challenged." The truth was that Jade's idea of investment was funding her latest home improvement project.

"Are you waiting on me?" The response to Rita's question was a swirl of hugs, no's, not-at-all's and so-glad-you-could-join-us, as she took the last chair at the table.

"How did it go with the kids?" Lori asked.

"Good. In fact, they've agreed to let me step in as CEO."

All mouths dropped, and all eyes stared at the announcement.

"CEO? Where did that come from?" Lori asked.

"According to Ned, SterTechCo is on the edge of financial disaster, and the kids would just as soon bail on the company. So I've taken a leave of absence from the station for the next couple of months, and we'll see what happens. At this point what do we have to lose?"

Jade spoke up. "But CEO? You have to admit, Rita, that's quite a leap."

"True, I don't have the background to pull it off alone, but I've never let that stop me before. Right? After all, what did I know about journalism when I got the job at the station?"

The friends raised their eyebrows and nodded their heads in unison while their server handed out a round of ice water.

"Lori, did you have time to look through the box?" Rita asked.

"I did, but I thought we were going to discuss that after lunch."

"I've been thinking about that, too. How long have we been friends?" Rita looked around the table. "Twenty years? Why haven't we ever talked about money?"

Marla squirmed and scrunched her face. "It's so personal."

"I didn't think we could get much more personal than the conversation we had about that *Sex and the City* episode a few weeks ago," Rita said.

Jade fanned herself with a napkin. "I second that."

The group fell in silent recollection of the discussion. Lori took a breath. "Rita, getting back to your question, there are lots of reasons women don't talk about money - lack of interest, no time. Or they may not know what they don't know and don't know who to ask. Or their comfort zone may revolve around the checkbook, and they're not willing to step outside it. Or like I mentioned yesterday, everything appears to be going well, so why get involved? Or maybe the wife voices a desire to participate, and the husband perceives it as questioning his ability."

"Maybe that's what was going on last night with Ned," Marla said. "I thought it was just business stress, but now I'm not sure. When I mentioned that I wanted to work together on the checkbook, he got defensive and locked himself in the den."

"I guess I haven't thought about money too much," Jade said. "I make it. I spend it. I have some taken out of my check toward my firm's 401k, but I couldn't tell you anything about my account."

Rita joined in. "It sounds like we all have a lot to learn about money in general and specifically about what's going on in our financial situations. I'm overwhelmed. I need help, and I don't have a lot of time. You're my friends. We have a resident financial planner. We could use our lunches as mini money workshops and work together on our financial issues, brainstorm solutions, learn from each other. How does that sound?"

Jade was quick. "I'm in."

"Sounds like a great idea," Lori said.

"Okay." Marla's lackluster tone pulled all eyes toward her.

"You told me you wanted to learn more about money," Lori said.

"Oh, I do. I just pictured going about it more anonymously."

"You're among friends," Lori reminded her.

"I know, but I'm not sure Ned will be thrilled about my discussing our financial situation with you guys."

Lori continued. "There's no pressure for you to divulge anything that makes you uncomfortable. Feel free to share whatever you want."

"Okay, then count me in." Her shoulders relaxed, and relief softened her face.

"Great," Rita said, "Now, Lori, what do you have to say about my personal finances?"

She dragged the box from under her chair and pulled out the top sheet. "Your intuition was correct. Cliff emptied out his brokerage account except for his IRA. That means that the only liquid assets – meaning money that you can get your hands on quickly – is whatever's in the checkbook, and that's about one month's worth of living expenses. Here, I did a cash flow statement." Lori handed it to Rita. "As you can see, I put your income at the top, then listed all the regular monthly expenses. For the time being I didn't include once-a-year bills like car registration and insurance or periodic amounts for such things as gifts, clothing, entertainment, etc." Rita's gaze hopped back and forth – item, amount, item, amount – until she got to the last two entries. Total expenses. She had no idea it cost that much to sustain their lives. Then she stared at the bottom line and the monthly deficit. The amount was big, double-underlined, and had a minus in front of it. A thought lingered for an extra second. Their lifestyle had dug them in deeper every month and yet, not a word from Cliff. There were her personal grooming services every month, regular meals at nice restaurants several times a week, little attention paid to the cost of groceries or decorating items for the house.

"But shouldn't we include those occasional expenses?" Jade interrupted

"Yes," Lori answered. "In fact, the non-monthly bills are usually the ones that set us up for budget failure, but considering Rita's immediate financial concerns, I focused on what's needed for the short-term." Lori turned her attention back to Rita. "Then there's the insurance money. That may take awhile. Have you contacted them?"

"No. I hadn't gotten around to that yet," Rita said. "I'll give them a call this afternoon and find out what I need to do."

Lori continued. "You have some breathing room for the moment, but obviously everything is riding on what happens with SterTechCo, because it has the potential to be your biggest asset and your best source of income. And we need to address the monthly deficit immediately."

"I haven't bought anything lately," Rita said. "Well, except I charged everything for Cliff's service."

The table fell silent while lunch was served.

"That's good," Lori said. "But obviously we need to look at all expenses moving forward to minimize the outgoing."

Marla leaned forward and spoke to Rita in a whisper. "I have to say I'm rather surprised. I thought that with the big house, nice cars and Cliff the CEO of a technology company, you were set financially."

"Trust me, you're not half as surprised as I am," Rita said. She then announced to her friends, "But I'm going to do whatever I can to turn the company around, and it starts first thing tomorrow. Brian, Christine and I are going to meet with the management team. I'll let you know how it went next time we get together."

"Speaking of which," Lori said to the group as they forked their entrees, "just like I did with Rita, the first step toward financial well-being is to find out where you are. So, Jade and Marla, your homework is to do an income and expense statement. I'll email you the form. Bring the completed statement next time, and we'll discuss what you learned from the process and how to use the information toward achieving your financial goals."

"Sounds good," Marla said as she glanced at her watch and patted her mouth with her napkin. She pulled a few bills from her wallet and dropped them in the middle of the table. "I didn't realize it was so late. I've got to pick up the kids. I'm excited about our new lunch topic. See you next week."

Lori raised her index finger and addressed the group. "Actually, how about we get together day after tomorrow? My office? Bring your lunch?"

"Works for me. See you then," Marla said as she waved goodbye

"Great idea." Jade rose and followed suit. "Bye."

Rita and Lori looked at each other.

"That was some lunch," Lori said.

"I was hoping for a little help from my friends. I didn't know I was going to start a movement."

"I'm so glad it turned out that way. For most women it's a question of when, not if, they're going to be in charge of their financial lives. We decide to remain single ... we get divorced ... we outlive our spouses."

"We take a lot for granted," Rita reflected.

"Until we're reminded how foolish that is," Lori finished.

---

*Go to the Appendix for a blank **Cash Income & Expenditures Statement**.*

Nine

Jade drummed her fingertips on the steering wheel while her focus darted between the traffic gridlock and her car's dashboard clock. A train ahead had cut off her most direct route to the office – again, which was going to make her late – again. She inched her way forward until a break in oncoming traffic made it possible for a quick left into Snob Hollow, an area that had been going through a rebirth of old mansions to office conversions. In her usual hurriedness Jade was about to roll through a stop sign when a car made a left turn in front of her, followed by a stream of westbound traffic.

"Great. Looks like everybody else had the same idea," she said to herself.

Her frustration soon changed to curiosity as her attention drifted to the corner property across the street. Surrounded by pristine professional buildings, it couldn't have looked more out of place. The short metal fence pushed against the sidewalk and drooped under the weight of overgrown shrubbery. Recent rain had papier-mached bits of trash along the bottom of the chain-link. In the slight morning breeze, tumbleweeds bounded around the yard like thorny sentinels, and a dense leafy web of tree branches rustled softly, allowing an occasional glimpse of the adobe structure beyond.

Jade glanced at her watch. "What are a couple more minutes?"

There was a break. She gunned the accelerator through the intersection, screeched to a halt, jumped out and headed toward a peeled-back section of fence on the west side, which looked like the cleanest access. She sucked in her breath and gingerly maneuvered sideways through the opening. Just as she had one foot in the yard, one of the branches she had pushed aside got loose and whacked its dusty leaves against her white linen sleeve, leaving a dark smudge. She silently reprimanded herself for not keeping a jumpsuit in the car.

She stood squarely in front of the house, arms crossed, eyes studying every inch of the structure as though she was double-checking a newly-completed set of blueprints. The paint was peeling, the porch and shutters sagged. But through Jade's eyes, its grandeur was only hiding. Good bones, she thought as her imagination righted the house's imperfections. She wondered about its history, how it ended up alone, what its future might hold. This house, my life ... Her mind wandered for a moment over the similarities.

She gave the notion a headshake and surveyed the obstacle course of dry-rot displayed on the porch. Three-inch heels would not have been her shoe of choice for this exploration, but Jade never let small technicalities get in her way. She tiptoed her way toward the large window to the left of the front door, finger-wiped the dusty film, cupped her hands to the glass, and strained to look inside. "Wow."

"It's really something, isn't it?" The voice startled her, and she knocked her forehead into the glass with a thunk. The tip of her stilettos caught in a hole in the floorboard, which sent her to the ground and on her butt with a solid thump.

"Are you all right?" A harmless-enough-looking man in his seventies, sporting cowboy boots and a Stetson, scurried over and helped her to her feet. "Didn't mean to scare you. Thought you heard me."

"I guess I was a little preoccupied. Sorry. I have a thing for old houses and can't seem to resist the impulse to snoop around. Are you the owner?" Jade asked as she dusted off the seat of her pants and retraced her route off the veranda.

"One of them." He extended his right hand. "Tony Atwood."

"Jade Hastings." She gave him a firm handshake.

"It was my mother's house. She died a couple of years ago ... three days after she'd turned 100. By golly, she was a determined woman – said she was going to live to be a hundred. I guess it just goes to show you what you can do when you put your mind to it." His smile broadened as he looked at the house. Then his gaze came back to Jade. "Anyway, I've been trying to settle the estate, but it's been one thing after another. Oh, listen to me carry on. Would you like a tour?"

"I'd love one."

"Let's go around to the back. It's a little less hazardous." He winked and motioned to a path through the knee-high grass, allowing Jade to lead the way. "I take it you work around here?"

"Yes. I'm an architect with Fenway & Finnegan over in the Arizona Bank building."

"No wonder you stopped. This building's a classic." A few steps later, he continued, "I thought maybe you were an attorney."

"I get that a lot. Not many female architects," Jade responded over her shoulder.

"Too bad ... I mean, you not being an attorney. Sure could use some help with the estate. The guy who was handling everything had a family emergency and ended up moving away. Can't say his partner has been all that interested."

"As it turns out, I'm doing a project for a lawyer who specializes in that area," Jade said. "I could give you a referral."

"I've got some paper and a pencil in the house. I'd sure appreciate that," Tony said.

Jade nodded in the direction of the carriage house. "There's a beauty. I don't think too many have survived around here."

"That's right. And even fewer have living quarters upstairs." Tony pointed to the top of the building.

"Looks like it's in pretty good shape." The hinges on the large wooden doors were rusty, and little paint was left attached to the structure; however, the windows were intact, and the wood appeared solid.

"Yeah, looks that way, but it hasn't had much attention for quite a while. Mom locked it up after Dad died, which was what?" Tony rubbed his chin in thought. "Maybe around twelve years ago now. I looked in there once after Mother died, then locked it back up. The place is full of junk. Dad collected old doorknobs, faucets, handles, lighting fixtures, and whatever else he could remove, using a screwdriver and a putty knife, while poking around abandoned houses in the neighborhood that were scheduled for demolition. Didn't know what he was going to do with them … just never wanted anything to go to waste, I guess." He fished a key out of his pocket and unlocked the back door.

A deep, four-legged, undivided sink stood underneath the window facing the backyard. Stand-alone cabinets filled in the spaces between the gold-colored stove and matching refrigerator. To her surprise the area was spick-and-span with a hint of disinfectant in the air. If she hadn't known better, she would have sworn someone had just gone down to the corner market.

As the two made their way through the opening into the next area, Jade's attention was drawn to the large crystal chandelier.

"Beautiful, isn't it?" Tony remarked. "Dad surprised Mom with that for her birthday. She loved anything glass, especially Depression glass. Ya know, the kind that turns purple. I swear there wasn't a piece made in that era that she didn't own at least one of. Dad even made her a special box with a black light to speed up the purpling process."

They continued on into the living room, which was outlined in wide crown molding and adorned with an intricately-carved cornice. The windows were original with wavy, bubbled glass, and the hardwood floors were worn but in excellent condition. "They don't build houses like this anymore," she said as she swiveled around on her heel. "All the attention to detail, and it's amazing how cool it is in here without air conditioning."

"And it wasn't until Mom got on in years, that us kids pitched in and got window units installed in the bedrooms. When Dad was alive, he was set against the idea. Too expensive to buy and operate," Tony said as he motioned toward the hall. "There are three bedrooms with the bathroom at the end."

They wandered in and out of the bedrooms, each containing the expected hardwood floors and tiny closets. The bathroom was adorned in pink and green tile. "Mom's idea," Tony said. "Dad was a plain-white kinda guy, but he left the decorating to Mom, and pink was her favorite color."

As the two made their way to the back door, Jade said, "It's a beautiful home. And in such great shape. It doesn't look as though you've had any vandalism, which is pretty amazing for an unoccupied house downtown."

He nodded. "We've been lucky. I get over here as often as I can, but my ranch is 45 minutes away. Over the years the trips into town have gotten fewer. My brother and sister live in Phoenix, so it's further yet for them. We hate to sell the place, but it doesn't work for any of us. Besides, it deserves someone who will enjoy it, take care of it."

"I didn't see a for sale sign," Jade said.

"There isn't one. One of those things I've been meaning to do. Been busy. And like I said, the attorney left, and I still need to clean out the carriage house. Besides, until recently, I guess we hadn't been ready to let it go," Tony said as he opened the drawer on the sideboard, fished out a piece of paper and a pencil, and handed them to Jade.

"Oh yeah, the attorney," she said as she began to write. "His name is Mark. I'll see him today and let him know you'll be calling. Oh, and let me give you my card, too."

"Thanks." Tony stuffed the paper and card into the breast pocket of his shirt, locked the door and pointed to a gate. "This will take us toward the street where we parked."

They walked in silence until they got to their cars. Tony extended his hand. "So nice to meet you. What good luck for me you like old houses."

"Good to meet you, too. Lucky for me you were such a good sport about me trespassing."

"Any time. The place hasn't seen such a beautiful woman since Mom died."

"Thank you." Jade blushed, got into her car, and waved goodbye out the window as she drove off.

What a gem, Jade thought as she continued toward work. And perfect for her first office rehab. She'd been itching for a project like this, a combination of the historical, residential remodels she'd done alongside her dad and her work as an architect in the area of new, commercial structures.

The euphoria of the find, however, lasted only until Jade parked in the underground garage. She let out a heavy sigh and stared at the concrete wall in front of her. What was she thinking? The notion of taking on a historical office space rehab at this time was ridiculous. The remodel on her home wasn't done. Time and money were scarce. The real estate market had been declining. Maybe there was more of her father in her than she was willing to admit. He was the dreamer; she, the practical one. Seconds ticked by as conflicting thoughts bounced between her brain's hemispheres, like a badminton birdie, before the last one landed on the side of reality. Jade shook off the visions of the Atwood house, opened the car door, grabbed her briefcase, and hoisted herself out of the car. Bad timing ... doesn't make sense ... too much to do ... she mumbled as she sprinted toward the stairwell.

Ten

Marla caught herself humming in mid-wipe as she scooped up the last of the morning's toast crumbs from the chipped, blue Formica. The previous day's discussion with her friends about finances had sparked new energy in Marla. She was excited again about learning how to cook for her family and practically giddy with the idea of redecorating the kitchen, which was going to be her first financial goal – a kitchen makeover good enough for a magazine shoot. She couldn't wait to share her dream with Ned. Maybe the discussion would get them reconnected again. Maybe she would even find out what had been bugging him lately.

"Where is everybody?" Ned made a beeline to the coffee pot.

"I got the boys ready early and over to Cindy's so that we won't be interrupted," Marla said.

He cocked his eyebrow. "What did you have in mind?"

"You promised we could go over our financial stuff together."

His expression turned cold. "Oh, that again. You know I'm jammed this time of year. Can't this wait?"

Marla stood firm. "Lori gave us homework over lunch yesterday – a cash flow statement – and we're going to talk about it tomorrow. Promise, this won't take long."

"Since when did homework become part of your lunches?" The furrows between his eyes deepened.

"Since we decided to make them mini money workshops."

"Wait a minute." Ned's tone was edgy. "Are you planning on sharing our personal information with your friends?"

"They said we didn't have to share, but … ."

Ned roared. "I don't like that one bit. I don't need a bunch of women critiquing how I manage our money. Besides, I'm an accountant. Don't you think I know a thing or two about money?"

"Of course you do. I'm not saying that."

"Don't you have enough to keep you busy without handling the finances, too?"

Courage and determination swelled. "It's not about taking over the finances or about having something else to do – it's about knowing what's going on. What's the big deal?"

Ned diverted his eyes to his coffee mug and hunched over it while the chicken clock on the wall ticked loudly in the overwhelming silence. "It's a long story," came out barely audible.

Marla sat down across from him. His face was a collage of emotions which confused her. "What's going on?"

More silence filled the room. Finally, he took a deep breath and looked into her eyes. "A while back I started trading stocks." Another deep breath. "In the beginning things were going very well … so good in fact that I wanted to do more, but I didn't have enough money. So I decided to borrow against the account to buy more stock. It's called 'margin.' It's great as long as the value of your portfolio stays the same or goes up; you just pay interest on the borrowed money, and you're fine. But if the value of the portfolio drops below a certain level, you get a margin call. Then you either have to come up with cash or sell some stock to cover the call. Are you with me so far?"

She nodded in understanding, but not in agreement. A sickening feeling was forming in the pit of her stomach.

Ned continued, looking past his wife to a spot on the wall behind her. "At one point we were millionaires." He allowed a heartbeat to pass, probably to let the idea sink in with Marla. "Then I started hearing about how you could make even more money buying and selling options." He avoided Marla's gaze. "Basically, you bet with someone that a stock is going to reach a certain price on a certain date."

"Sounds hard," Marla said. "And risky."

"If you know what you're doing, you can make some significant money," Ned said. "I went to one of those seminars, and it was amazing. The instructor made real money right in front of us. I was hooked. I signed up for the program and began making trades … a few with small amounts of money, and they were successful."

Marla held her breath. She sensed the impending doom.

"Work got crazy, so I spent less time watching the market and our holdings. I thought I could get away with a few hours here and there, but I was wrong. The market began to slide, and our stocks along with it; then came the margin calls. If I had been more attentive, maybe I would have bought protection in the form of put options or even sold short, but I didn't."

Marla's head was spinning. Sliding markets? Millionaires? Margin calls? Options? "Didn't we only lose what we really didn't have? Kinda like playing with the house's money when you're gambling?"

Ned shook his head. "If only I had lost the paper profits, I'd be happy." He paused. "I lost everything, including the initial investment plus I had to pay the margin interest."

Lost everything. The words knocked her back in her chair. The clock ticked through the silence and ratcheted up emotions from disbelief and confusion to anger. "I can't believe what I'm hearing! How could you do such a thing without ever discussing it with me?"

"You told me when we first got married that you weren't interested in anything financial, so honestly, I didn't think about talking it over with you." There was a slight undertone of defiance in his voice.

"I wouldn't put gambling with our family's future in the same realm as most financial matters." Marla fumed. "So, where are we exactly?"

Ned got up from the table, walked to the coffee pot and refilled his mug. After a few moments he turned to Marla. "Around $200 in savings … and the credit cards are maxed out."

"How did that happen? The credit cards?" The shrill tone surprised both of them.

Ned took his seat again at the kitchen table and lowered his gaze to the floor. "I'm so sorry." He shook his head. "Right before all the investment stuff went downhill, the word came down from the senior partner that he wanted us to hold positions in various professional organizations, said the recognition would look good on the lobby walls. Anyway, that meant a lot of schmoozing for votes – dinners, drinks, and entertainment perks. Unfortunately, he didn't volunteer to pick up the tab for most of that, and I didn't want to ask him to reimburse me because I didn't want him to think I couldn't afford it. It was expensive." He let out a sigh. "At the same time we had a few emergencies around here. Remember the roof leak, the broken pipe outside and the refrigerator all went out at once?"

She nodded.

"With nothing left in savings I had no choice but to charge everything, and I've been making minimum payments ever since."

The news was making her dizzy. "How long were you planning on keeping all of this a secret from me? How long were you planning on living this lie?"

The heavy exhale sounded like it contained years' worth of stress and frustration. "I don't know. I thought it would start to come together and I wouldn't have to. But I'm glad everything is out in the open now, I really am." Ned looked into her eyes. "I'm so sorry."

"Sorry" was a good start, but it didn't quash her anger. She had trusted him to take care of them. Now her head was drowning in questions about their future.

Ned checked the clock. "Marla, I've got to get to work."

She pushed aside her fear. "I need to know what's going on. I need specifics."

His gaze darted between the door and the clock. "And we'll go over everything when tax season is over. Promise."

"But what about my homework?" Marla pressed.

Ned set his jaw and struck a wide-eyed stare at his wife. Then his shoulders slumped. "Uh, okay." He hurried down the hall and returned with a stack of papers, topped with the checkbook. "Here you go. And

I've got to go. I'll call you later." A peck on her cheek, and he was of the house and backing down the driveway in his car.

~

Across town Jade was unearthing her own financial reality. High from a pot of coffee, she surveyed the neatly stacked piles of statements on the living room's carpet. Not surprising the number of remodeling invoices towered above the rest. She wondered. *Did she have the makings of a present-day version of Mrs. Winchester who built on her house 24/7 for 38 years?* According to legend, for the Widow Winchester the constant construction was about appeasing the victims of her husband's guns. For Jade it was about taking up her presently unoccupied relationship time.

The yellow legal pad recorded the monthly expenses per Lori's form – utilities, food, eating out … wow, that was a chunk … car payment, house payment, home equity line of credit, personal stuff. Then there was the staggering construction total. What was that exactly? Entertainment? Sometimes. Home repairs? The projects had blown past that description years ago. Therapy? Not in the true medical sense of the word – but it should be.

She chewed on her upper lip while staring at the numbers. Setting aside construction costs, the bottom line didn't look *too* bad. But, for her income, she should have more to show for it. And everything was tied to her ability to earn a living. What if something happened to her and she couldn't work? How would she pay her bills? The answers sent a shiver up her spine.

Go to the Appendix for the article entitled **Options – and the Trading of Them.**

Eleven

No sooner had Rita stopped her luxury sedan in the SterTechCo parking lot, than fear flooded her system. What was she thinking? What was she doing there? No experience. No qualifications. No background. Turn around and go home. Do something else.

Her eyes clouded behind a film of tears. She took a deep breath and stared across the empty asphalt. How ironic. Twenty-five years ago she sat in the same parking lot, mustering enough courage to get out of the car to begin her first day of work at Fortuna Properties, a real estate development company. At the time she was a stringy, blonde-haired sixteen-year-old with no office experience, few secretarial skills and even less business etiquette. But the gray-haired founder and CEO took a chance on her for an "assistant to an admin assistant" position, and everybody thought he was crazy. Today the best she could hope for as the new CEO was that the SterTechCo management team didn't think *she* was crazy.

Rita opened the door, planted her three-inch heels firmly on the ground and pulled herself out of the car. The stakes were high, and she felt the pressure. Twenty-five years ago it was about getting a job so she could make her car payment; today it was about saving other people's jobs so they could make their house payments. Rita took a deep breath and headed toward the elevator. Its doors opened, and she pushed the fifth-floor button.

Recently, SterTechCo had leased the same space Fortuna had occupied. In many ways it was home. She learned her work ethic there and watched the American dream in progress. However, about the time Rita resigned to attend college, tension along with declining home sales had replaced enthusiasm at Fortuna. Layoffs came, building contracts became worthless, and lawsuits ensued. Within one year of the founder's death, Fortuna had to close its doors. Rita couldn't let the same demise come to the company Cliff had worked so hard to build. The elevator doors opened and she hurried toward Cliff's office. Along the way she was met with polite hellos and puzzled faces. Rita reciprocated with smiles until she arrived at Carmen's desk, located in a small cubicle outside Cliff's office. Carmen was in her early 60's with salt-and-pepper hair and freckles. Her eyes were unusually puffy, her skin splotchy. Cliff's death had hit her quite hard. She'd been his assistant since the company's early days in his garage, two years before Rita met Cliff.

"Oh, Rita," Carmen said. "What a pleasant surprise to see you. How are you doing?" She diverted her bloodshot eyes and quickly tossed a crumpled Kleenex into the wastebasket.

"I'm hanging in there." Rita shrugged. "I still expect for Cliff to walk in the door any minute. Crazy, huh?"

"No, same here." The two women fell in awkward silence for a moment.

"So, how are things going around here?" Rita asked.

"For everybody else, it's pretty much business as usual," Carmen replied. "For me, it's been rather quiet. I field some questions; the rest I forward to Glen. I've filed everything." She glanced at the cabinets. "Of course we're all wondering what's going to happen."

"Christine and Brian are meeting me here shortly, and that's what we're going to talk about," Rita told her. "I'm going to wait for them in there." She motioned with her head toward Cliff's office.

She walked reverently toward his desk, stood on the visitor's side, and surveyed the top of the workspace. It didn't appear Carmen had moved so much as a piece of paper – orderly stacks of reports and correspondence, appointment book open to the week he died, the bottom of his coffee mug stained with his remnants of its last cup. Gently running her fingertips along the edge of the dark mahogany, Rita made her way around one corner, then the next until she stood behind the desk and in front of his black leather, high-back executive chair. She eased her way onto the seat, closed her eyes, and gently wiggled to see if it would fit. It didn't. Would it ever?

"Here you are." The words startled Rita. Her eyes opened, and she shot out of the chair as Brian and Christine closed the door behind them.

"Sorry." Rita's face pinked as though she was caught misbehaving.

"No worries," Brian said as he motioned for her to sit down. "You have every right to be there. You're the CEO."

"Oh, I know." Embarrassment still warmed her cheeks. She glanced at the chair. "Maybe this is a big mistake."

Christine looked at her brother, then at Rita. "The mistake would be not giving this idea all we've got. Otherwise, we might as well go home now."

"I agree," Brian said. "None of us want to be in this situation, but we are, and we've got to give this plan our best shot." When Rita and Christine nodded, he arched a brow. "Let's put together our thoughts before the meeting."

The threesome gathered around the coffee table in the sitting area to the side of the desk. Brian began. "I'm sure everyone is anxious about what's going to happen now, so I think the first course of business should be to share what we've discussed, deal with any fallout, then request a status report or state of the company. Specifically, what are the financials not telling us?"

"Sounds like a plan," Rita said as she leaned her ear toward the conference room. "I hear some voices next door. I guess it's show time."

They walked through the adjoining door and were met with handshakes and the usual business pleasantries, but furrowed eyebrows and some awkwardness toward the family conveyed the group's concern. Glen nodded to Kerry, the implementation manager, and Michelle, the office manager and bookkeeper, and gestured in a gentlemanly manner to the chairs at the table across from the Sterlings. Glen followed the two women, and Saleem, the development manager, closed the door behind them.

To say the least, the group was diverse. Kerry had massive, curly, shoulder-length brown hair; big, brown eyes adorned in heavy mascara; plump, pouty lips; a medium-plus frame; and a voice that rarely needed a microphone. Half Kerry's size, Michelle was a little older with gel-spiked, light brown hair; narrow, gray-brown framed glasses; and more chest than hips. Saleem was from India by way of Canada. He was on the shorter side of average height and on the softer side of muscle-bound. Glen had been an athlete all his life, and it showed. The sports may have changed over the years as joints and muscle groups were challenged, but there was no doubt that exercise was a constant in his daily routine.

Everyone quickly settled into a seat, leaving the chair at the head of the table empty. Drawing on her many years in front of the camera, Rita looked each person in the eye and took a breath. This was live. No editing, no going back.

"I'm sure you've been wondering what's going to happen to SterTechCo now that Cliff is gone." She paused. "His will provided that his shares be divided equally among the three of us. We've talked." She nodded to the kids. "And let me assure you it's our goal to keep the company going." Rita paused for a collective sigh of relief. "Brian and Christine are happy in their current professional pursuits and aren't interested in coming back here full time; however, they have agreed to consult with me on an as-needed basis as I take on the responsibilities of CEO." She stopped. Gazes darted between members of the management team.

Glen broke the silence. "I'm sure I speak for everyone when I say that *surprised* would be an understatement."

"I know I have a lot to learn, but I love this company, and I want to make it work. I know you all do, too," Rita said to each of them.

Glen rested his elbows on the table, laced his fingers together and leaned toward Rita. His expression softened; his words grew almost patronizing. "I'm not disputing your intentions, but it's going to take more than good intentions to run this company." He leaned back in his chair and crossed his arms. When he continued, the tone was strained. "You know, Cliff and I go way back. I've been here from the beginning, through everything. I thought I would be the logical choice for CEO … I guess I was wrong." He paused. "Maybe it's time for me to move on."

A wave of panic came over Rita. *No, no, no*, she screamed in her head as she sat poised and demurred.

Brian jumped in. "Glen, let's not be hasty. While technically Rita is the CEO, we're utilizing a team management approach, and of course we want you to be part of that team. Besides, you still hold the largest number of shares outside of the three of us, so you have a lot at stake here."

Glen allowed a few moments to pass before responding. "Alright, let's see how things go." He gave a slight shrug. "I promise to stay at least long enough to get through this rough spot."

The atmosphere in the room relaxed. Rita could breathe … and speak … again. "Thank you, Glen, I really appreciate that." Then she addressed the group. "Our immediate concern is that SterTechCo only has enough cash reserves to cover expenses for the next two months. Obviously, that's not much time. Kerry, where do we stand on current projects?"

Kerry sat tall and referred to the paper in front of her. "A couple are close to completion. All we're waiting on is for Saleem to fix some engineering glitches in the program."

Saleem looked at Kerry. "You say engineering glitches; I say your department's programming inadequacies. We must move on to the next version, not spend all our time fixing the old," he retorted in a thick Indian accent.

Kerry made eye contact with Christine. "As you can hear, nothing's changed since you left."

Glen said to Saleem and Kerry, "Okay, you two." He turned his attention to Rita. "Cliff probably told you how it worked around here, but to bring you up to speed, Saleem's department creates the software. Once the contract is signed, Kerry's department integrates the software into the clients' technology, which requires some customization. The constant challenge for Kerry's group is allocating man-hours between completing current projects utilizing the latest version of the software, which often needs program corrections to operate properly, and supporting previous versions, which require regular adjustments as client needs change. The higher payoff is the completion of new contracts, but customer satisfaction on the maintenance side is critical to our reputation and future business. Saleem believes his function is to create new versions, and adjustments to older versions should be done by Kerry's team."

Kerry interjected. "Which is why we get so bogged down. By the time we get the software, it should be ready for integration. We shouldn't have to rewrite most of the code to make it work properly."

"*Research and development* is just that," Saleem defended. "We look forward, not backward."

Bits and pieces of Cliff's daily ramblings about work began to come into mental focus as Rita listened to Saleem and Kerry volley accusations. The feud between the departments had been going on for as long as she could remember. At his wit's end, her husband added "Operations Manager" to Glen's duties in the hope that a new approach might bring a truce. Six months later apparently nothing had changed.

"The way I see it," Rita began, "we either decide to work together or we might as well shut our doors right now." Eyes remained glued on Rita. "Good. I'll take that silence to mean we're going to work together. Saleem and Kerry, please discuss with your teams how we're going to meet delivery deadlines so we can get paid and keep this company afloat. We'll reconvene in the next day or so to develop our game plan. Any questions?"

Glances ricocheted off of one another and ended back at Rita.

"Cliff was proud of all of SterTechCo employees, and he believed they had the individual talent to do anything," Rita continued, making eye contact with each person at the table. "What each individual must decide now is whether to share their talent for the greater good or take their talent elsewhere." She allowed the words to sink in. "Glen, do you have a few moments?"

"Sure."

Rita addressed the group. "Then we're adjourned."

Glen was staring out the large plate glass window when Rita closed the door. She had known him almost as long as she had known Cliff, but their relationship had shifted in the boardroom.

"I probably should have called you about the CEO decision," Rita said, walking toward him. "But everything is happening so fast. I apologize for springing it on you during the meeting."

He didn't move. "We never actually talked about who would run SterTechCo in the event something happened to him, but since I was second in command, so to speak, I thought it was a given." He turned to face Rita. "I can understand that Cliff may have wanted to keep the company in the family, but ownership and leadership are two different issues. I don't think he envisioned you in a management position."

Men had been quick to judge her through her whole life based on her beauty, including Cliff until their first date when they ended up discussing micro and macro economics until three in the morning. Even though Rita's father never finished high school, he was well-read, and the two of them often debated a variety of topics. Constant reading had been her only defense.

"Maybe, maybe not," Rita said, "You've only known me as Cliff's wife and a pretty face on the news."

Glen cocked his eyebrow.

Rita blew out a sigh. "I *do* have a brain."

"Hold on now. I did not say you didn't," Glen said. "It's just that being *in* the trenches is quite different than hearing *about* the trenches over dinner. And we're in crisis mode. I would venture to say that even the most experienced manager would be challenged in this environment."

He had a point. There was knowledge, then there was application. She had a little of the former, none of the latter. Rita needed him on board all the way, not just going through the motions. She and the kids hadn't talked about this, but she needed to sweeten the pot. She motioned to a couple of chairs and they sat down across from one another. "I may not know the business like you and Cliff, but I *do* know he believed in the product and this company – so much so that he invested everything he had, we had, in this business." *Probably even his life*, she thought, and took a breath. "There's no disputing the fact that you're more suitable to run SterTechCo, but my whole financial life is riding on saving this company, and I can't sit at home and wait for something to happen. So, here's what I propose: you and I work together to get SterTechCo back on track, and I'll talk to the kids about giving you more company stock."

Traffic noise wafted through the air while seconds ticked by. Glen stood up and extended his hand. "You've got a deal."

Rita jumped up, shook his hand, then gave him a quick hug. "Great!" She glanced at the wall clock. "I've got to get to an appointment. Let's get together with Brian and Christine after lunch in Cliff's office."

He nodded.

"Good. I'll see you then," she said, dashing next door to retrieve her purse. By the time she reached the elevator, her heart and head were pounding. The ride on the internal emotional rollercoaster had been exhausting. Doubt – will the money come through to keep SterTechCo going? Fear – what will she do if it doesn't? Self-doubt – had she overstepped her bounds by offering the company stock without discussing the idea with Brian and Christine? Anger – why did Cliff have to die now?

Tears began to swell. The elevator doors opened. Rita hurried onboard, pushed the ground floor button, then the button to close the doors. *Hurry, hurry.* She pushed the button. *I can't hold them back. I don't want anybody to see me cry.*

Twelve

Rita sat quietly in Lori's conference room while Lori and Marla talked. On the one hand, she didn't want to be there – pressing matters at SterTechCo were consuming her thoughts. On the other hand, she needed to learn about personal finances. There was no time to waste.

"Thanks for making this a brown-bag lunch," Jade said as she rolled her chair closer to the large, glass-topped table where her other three friends were already seated. "I don't know about the rest of you, but my budget could use a break from dining out. Did I miss anything?"

"No, everybody just got here." Lori peeled off large sheets of Post-It paper and passed them around along with large markers. "Let's copy our cash flow statements onto these. We'll put them up and see what's going on with everybody."

In between bites from Tupperware dishes, the group busied themselves by transferring numbers, and soon each of them had tacked their work on the walls.

"Who wants to start?" Lori asked. "Marla, how about you?"

"I don't know if you want to start with me. I'm a mess."

"Come on, it can't be that bad," Jade said.

"How about broke?"

"Really?" Rita asked.

"Actually, more than broke." Marla said.

"How can that be?" Rita was surprised. Besides Lori and Bob, Marla and Ned would have been her next best guess for the most financially-together couple.

"If you've got a whole lot more going out than you've got coming in, you're more than broke," Marla answered with a slight tremble.

"So, which sheet is yours?" Lori asked

Marla pointed to it, and the group's eyes scanned line-by-line until the big minus sign in front of the bottom number. "I take it that you and Ned have talked about this?"

"More or less." Marla sighed. "He confessed that a couple of years ago he was trading stocks on margin and lost everything. Then he went to some seminar and started trading options." Her expression soured as though a foul odor had whiffed by. "Expenses started piling up, so he began to charge everything. The cards are all maxed out, and he's been making only minimum payments for the last year." She paused. "On top of that he's been playing a shell game with the credit cards to keep us afloat … you know, transferring balances to new cards for a low interest rate."

"Which isn't necessarily a bad idea," Lori interrupted, "but it's important to read the fine print on those offers."

"Tell me about it," Marla continued. "We're paying about 21% on most of our cards, so the best we can do is make minimum payments."

Lori surveyed the remaining sheets, then addressed the group. "Glancing at the rest of our sheets, I see that it looks like we all can use some discussion about getting rid of credit card debt. What can we do to pay them off as soon as possible?"

"I've been looking at which expenses I can cut so my cash will last longer," Rita said. "Wouldn't the same idea apply … freeing up money going out for certain expenses and putting it to the credit cards?"

"Absolutely," Lori said. "What types of expenses could we reduce or eliminate?"

Jade was quick. "Non-essentials. I would guess pretty much anything other than mortgage and car payments, utilities, food, etc."

"Right," Lori said. "As we study these, where could we make adjustments?"

Rita piped in. "I've decided to eliminate mani's and pedi's and eating out. Trips to the mall are on hiatus indefinitely. I've scaled back to basic cable, and I'm going to inquire how I can reduce my cell phone bill." All of that was well and good, she thought, but the changes did little to reduce the significant negative bottom line. They had lived well – too well – and now she was afraid how that was going to affect her future.

"All that sounds great," Lori said. "The severity of our cash flow situation dictates how many and to what degree expenses must be adjusted or eliminated."

Rita frowned. "But some things are sacred, right? Like, our houses?"

Lori shook her head. "Not necessarily. Depending on how dire a person's financial situation is, every expense is up for grabs, including our homes. For example, what if the decision was to move to an apartment to get rid of a mortgage payment or to be homeless?" The room turned somber. "Luckily, from the looks of these, none of us are in that situation right now, but when it comes to finances, we must be constantly vigilant." Lori turned to Marla. "What did you and Ned decide about your situation?"

"*He* decided we would talk about it after tax season. *I've* decided there are some areas where we can make changes. We eat out a lot, so I'm going to learn to cook … for real this time. I know, I've said that before, but I'm serious. And I'm open to suggestions. I don't want to spend the money on a class, but I can't even follow a recipe."

"I'll give you some pointers," Lori volunteered.

"I know a few things about cooking. I'm happy to share," Rita chipped in.

"Thanks so much, guys. You're the best." Marla returned to her list. "Other than that, I Googled 'money savings ideas' and got some great ideas on how to save on utilities, entertainment, and at the grocery store. Unfortunately, I think I'm still going to be in the red."

"We'll get back to that in a minute," Lori said. "Jade, what did you find out about your situation?"

Jade gulped her mouthful of salad and dabbed her lips. "Obviously, I've been spending most of my money on renovations, but I had no idea what all of that was costing until I went through the numbers. So, I'm going to finish what I have to on the house and call it done. I did an inventory of materials and discovered that I have everything I need to complete the projects in progress. I've also decided to put the brakes on my fluff spending."

"Does that include your daily Venti, Mocha Frappuccino, double-blended?" Rita asked with a smile.

Jade sighed. "Sad, but true."

"How will we be able to recognize you without that cardboard coffee cup in your hand?"

Lori piped in. "Actually, making minor changes in our daily habits, such as skipping a cup of designer coffee, can make a huge difference in the long run. Let's add it up." She grabbed her HP calculator and started pushing buttons. "$4.00 a day times ... 5 days a week ... times 52 weeks equals $1,040."

"Wow," the group whispered.

Lori pushed more buttons. "If you think that's 'wow,' then let's say we invest that money at 8% for 20 years. You'd have almost $51,400."

"That's amazing," Marla said.

"That's called the compounding effect of money," Lori said. "Awesome, isn't it?" She allowed a few clicks of the clock to pass. "I guess that just leaves my monthly statement. As you were going through your check registers and credit card statements, you may have noticed how the *non-monthly* expenses – such as clothing, large purchases, car repairs, gifts, and in my case, Bob's big-boy-toy addiction – can have a significant effect on the overall budget."

Marla agreed. "Can it ever. I've got a techno-geek on my hands. Talk about expensive gadgets!"

"That must be tough to deal with ... spouses having different ideas when it comes to what to do with their money," Jade said.

"You're right," Lori said, "How we should spend or save our money is the biggest challenge in our marriage, along with most couples. We're so far apart that presently, we're negotiating our way onto the same bookshelf with the hope of one day getting on the same page."

"At least Bob hasn't tried to hide his financial habits." Marla took a breath. "I feel like Ned cheated on me financially, keeping secrets. Does that make sense?"

Lori nodded her head. "I've heard it called 'financial infidelity,' and it's more common than you may think. If a partner isn't involved in the couple's finances, who knows what the other one is doing. And with that can come devastating consequences."

Rita had full blown consequences, and it scared the hell out of her. There was so much to learn. A day at a time … a day at a time … the mantra played in her head.

"Well, I'm involved now," Marla said, a furrow appearing on her forehead. "Getting back to paying off the credit cards, does it make any difference if we pay on each one equally or try to pay off one at a time?"

Jade stopped in mid-chew. "I think paying the ones off with the highest rate would make the most sense, right?"

"That method gives you the greatest benefit because you end up paying less interest," Lori agreed. "What's another approach?"

The group played with their food. "What if you paid off the one with the smallest balance first, regardless of the interest rate?" Rita asked. The question was met with inquisitive stares from Jade and Marla.

"Go ahead," Lori encouraged, smiling.

Rita drew out her response. "I was just thinking … if you paid one card off, you'd feel a sense of accomplishment, and it would encourage you to pay off the next one and the next one, until they are all paid off."

"You're right. There's a sort of instant gratification to that method," Lori said. "No matter which way you go, the important point is that you pay as much as you can without adding any more debt. After all, it doesn't do us any good if we're charging as much, or more, as we're paying every month."

Jade raised a finger to be recognized. "If we have equity in our home, wouldn't it be easier and quicker to pay everything off with a line of credit or second mortgage?"

"Personally, I view that option as least attractive for two reasons," Lori began. "I don't like to see people putting their home at risk for consumer debt. First, fluctuations in the real estate market can create situations where if we had to sell, we could owe more than it's worth. And secondly, it's been my experience that if we don't change our spending habits or attitudes about money, we could end up in the same situation, only with an additional mortgage payment. We would be even deeper in debt and have fewer options."

Lori let the idea sink in before she continued. "Besides reducing expenses, what else can we do to have money left over after the bills have been paid?"

"Increase income," Rita answered.

"Good," Lori said. "Marla, have you and Ned talked about that?"

"No, but I think he could network to drum up new clients ... maybe teach at the community college."

"Is there something *you* can do?" Lori asked.

Marla tipped her head to the side, tapped her temple, and stared at the group. Seconds clicked by. "I hadn't thought about that." The words were slow and drawn out. "I've been a wife and mother since graduation, and I'm not sure what I can do with a bachelor's degree in social work."

Rita spoke up. "You're selling yourself short. There are opportunities everywhere if you look for them."

"I agree," Jade said. "You don't need to limit your search to social work. What else interests you? Look around. Be creative. Be open. You might be surprised with what you find."

Marla nodded.

"Wow! There's some inspiration," Lori said, glancing at the wall clock "What a great stopping place for today. Not bad for our first money workshop, huh?" Enthusiastic nods and smiles swept around the table. "How about we get together a couple of times a week to keep this momentum going?" Universal agreement continued. "Okay, I have a few assignments. For our next meeting I'd like each of us to come up with at least one money-generating idea to increase our incomes, and also to complete a Balance Sheet, which I'll give you before you go." Everyone nodded as they began to gather papers and lunch remnants. "Oh, one more thing ... I'd like us to go cash-only for a week, which means no charging. Then we'll talk about what effect that had on our spending."

Marla stopped mid-cleanup. "I'm not sure Ned is going to go along with that. According to him, we've been pretty much living on credit," she said to Lori.

"I'm not expecting Bob to jump on the bandwagon either, but talk it over with Ned and see if you can work out a compromise."

Marla shrugged and nodded.

"Great," Lori said. "I'll be right back with the Balance Sheets for everyone." By the end of the sentence Lori was in the copy room, and moments later she was handing them out along with a good-bye hug.

---

*Go to the Appendix for a blank **Balance Sheet** and articles:*
***How to Increase Your Cash Flow Bottom Line** and*
Starr's Fifty Favorite Money-Saving Ideas.

Thirteen

What can I do? What can I do? What can I do? The words spun through Marla's head as she drove home from Lori's office.

She dropped her purse and keys on the kitchen counter and checked the digital clock on the microwave. Good. An hour before the kids got home.

She snatched the newspaper from the kitchen table, added it to the Balance Sheet Lori had given her, and made her way into the living room. Marla settled into her favorite spot on the sofa, clicked the remote to the HGTV channel, and opened the newspaper to the classifieds. Even though she was a glass-half-full kind of person, she was also a realist. She had a 20-year-old bachelor's degree in social work and no work experience at anything outside of the home. When Ned and Marla got married, the plan was that she would get her Masters after the kids went to school, but at this point an advanced degree or any other degree, for that matter, was too far off to do anything positive for their situation now. The best she could hope for was something she could do to bring in some money until they could afford for her to go back to school.

Marla took a deep breath and began to read. *Administrative/Professional.* Wrong degree. Not enough education. No experience. *Leasing Consultant. Family Support Specialist.* Red circles, possibilities. *Education. Teaching positions.* Talk to Ned. Maybe he could teach an accounting or tax class. *Clerical/Office. Receptionist.* Computer skills required. She didn't have any. The paper crumpled in her hands as it dropped onto her lap. Who was going to hire her?

In the midst of a brief moment of self-pity, the show *Sell This House* caught her attention. It had always been one of her favorite shows, but if she didn't get busy, it was going to become her reality.

Marla folded the paper so that the circled ads glared at her. She headed to the family computer in a corner of the breakfast nook and powered up the machine. Once on the Google search page, she typed "jobs" and was instantaneously presented with millions of hits. She chose a website she had seen advertised on TV. The screen asked for location … that was easy … Tucson. Over 500 positions popped up. The total number of jobs looked promising, but by the time she had scrolled to page ten, her enthusiasm had begun to wane. *Sales. Technical. Engineers. Health Care. Extensive travel. Bilingual.* The positions were out of her league and out of reach. There were a few listings for survey takers. She'd come back to those. Another website proved to be the same – hundreds of positions for which she was not qualified.

The back door opened.

"Knock, knock," Rachel called as Marla's twin boys ran in and hugged their mom. Rachel's son stuck to his mother's leg like a wet tongue on a new popsicle. Marla and Rachel had met during a kindergarten mixer at their sons' school and soon became friends and carpool buddies.

"Come in," Marla said. "How was school today, you two?"

They both started talking at once. "Way cool. Ramon brought in a lizard he found, and it got away. He couldn't catch it, and Mrs. Moore was screaming. Yeah, and Jason's nose started bleeding, and there was blood everywhere, and he had to go to the nurse's office, and the guy came in and cleaned up the blood. It was so cool."

Marla nodded. Her gaze darted between the boys while they gushed out the news of the day. "Is Jason okay?"

"Yeah, yeah. His nose bleeds all the time," Zane said.

"Why don't all you guys go play for a couple of minutes while I talk to Mrs. Rodriguez," Marla said.

Zach's eyes widened. "Come on, Carlos," he said in tones spiked with excitement. "We'll show you the neat fort we just got. Our dad put it together."

"Wait, wait, wait," Marla called to the back of their heads as they ran through the living room. "Lost cause. Do you have a few minutes?"

"Sure," Rachel replied.

"We can sit and watch the boys play." The two friends snaked through the living room, passing between the leather sectional and the entertainment center brimming with the latest electronics. The 60" plasma TV was framed with shelves lined with DVDs, CDs, video games, a TiVo box, surround-sound and audio equipment.

They settled into the plush outdoor dining set on the back porch. "That's quite a set-up," Rachel remarked as they watched the boys climb, slide and crawl around the large wooden fort replica, which had been sandwiched between the above-ground pool and jungle-gym.

"Yes, it is," Marla said. Her stomach tightened. Ned's latest addition to their mounting credit card balances. "I've been thinking about getting a job. You know, while the boys are at school."

"Me, too," Rachel said. "They always need help on the playground and in the classrooms. I was going to look into that. We could do it together."

"I love kids and I love my boys, but I think I'd like to be around adults for a change," Marla said. "Although I'm not sure exactly what I want to do. I guess you can say I'm in the research stage ... looking in the newspaper, on the Internet."

"Yeah, I know what you mean," Rachel said. "I wouldn't mind something different, but what?"

Minutes ticked by while the two women sat deep in thought. "You know, when I was in college, I remember filling out a personal inventory assessment." Her friend's face grew curious. "The one I'm thinking of was on an actual form, but we could make something similar that might help us. I'll grab some paper." Marla dashed into the house and returned a short time later with pen and paper for each of them.

"You make four columns: one for hobbies and interests; one for talents and abilities; one for experience; and one for education," Marla instructed as she drew lines and titled each column. Rachel followed suit. "There are no rules for this. You can put whatever comes to mind in each column. It doesn't have to be work-related. The idea is to allow the brain to make a connection between two ideas that it maybe wouldn't have made otherwise."

"I'm game," Rachel said, and both women began to write.

"Hey, Mom, we're hungry," yelled Zane.

"Okay, let's go in the house," Marla answered, then said to Rachel, "You can take it home, and we can talk about it later if you want."

"Let's do that," Rachel said as they gathered the papers and followed the boys through the sliding door toward the kitchen. "Carlos, we need to get home."

"Ah, Mom, can't I stay just a little longer?" he begged.

"I've got a lot to do before your dad gets home. You can come back another time."

Carlos slouched and began to drag his feet slowly toward the door.

"Thanks," Rachel said. "I'll give you a call."

They gave each other a hug, and Rachel closed the door behind her. Marla picked an apple from the refrigerator vegetable bin, cleaned it, cut and cored it, and gave the twins half each. "Can we eat these in the living room and color, Mom?" Zach asked.

"Yes, and take a napkin," Marla said as they obeyed and ran out of the kitchen.

Marla went to the den, gathered the recent statements she had worked on, and propped herself on the couch with her financial homework and personal inventory sheet. The television hummed with more decorating tips. The project on the screen caught her attention. *That wall art they've created really brings the room together. And it's so easy and inexpensive. I could to do that. First though … .* She pulled out the personal inventory sheet and added "art" and "decorating" to the "talents" category. A survey of her attributes, interests and education netted a whole lot of *gee-that's-nice*, but no concrete anything she could build on to get much of a job.

She picked up the blank Balance Sheet along with their statements and went to work. Minutes later the form's bottom line confirmed her fear that it was as dismal as the Cash Flow Statement. There was a little home equity, a small amount in Ned's retirement plan at work, but between the mortgages and credit cards, their grand total net worth was zero … and that was being somewhat optimistic about the value of their home. How could they work all these years and end up with essentially nothing financially?

"Mom, come color with us." Zane rattled her thoughts back to the present.

"Okay, you guys," Marla said, crawling onto the carpet and picking up a coloring book. As she leafed through the pages, a thought began to form. An idea hit her. Yes, that had potential. That could work. Yes, yes, yes … . She bolted off the floor and ran to the computer.

~

While a multi-colored ball ricocheted on Jade's computer screen, and blueprints for the Tremoline project lay dormant on the drafting table, Jade contemplated her life. Delving into her fiscal irresponsibility had begun to raise deeper questions. *Who am I?* Besides a divorced architect, who found old buildings more interesting than most men she met, who had worked for the same firm since college. *What do I want?* Independence to work on projects of her choosing, to create an income stream from investment properties so she didn't have to work for someone else. *What's my purpose?* To rehab, recycle, rejuvenate, to bring new life to old storefronts and factories which have stood dead for too many years. Becoming an architect was the perfect combination of her love of buildings and art, and creating was as vital to Jade as breathing. But years of cookie-cutter professional plazas and nitpicky homeowners had left her going through the motions. The Atwood home. She couldn't get the property out of her mind. Yes, they needed each other, a chance at a new life – for the house, a new purpose as an office; for Jade, the first step toward doing historic commercial on her own and her first investment income property. Somehow, she had to make it work. The question was: how?

Jade pulled out the papers from the lunch meeting with the girls and began to work on the two worksheets. The real estate market had been soft lately, but maybe there was a little equity to pull out from her house, especially with the improvements she'd made since she bought it. She could cut personal expenses and eating out. There was her company's retirement plan ... no, can't do that. Jade blew out a sigh. So much had changed in lenders' loan policies since she purchased her home a couple of years ago. Was there enough of anything to meet the new criteria? Even if she could come up with the down payment, what about the renovation costs? *Think. Think. Think.*

Her cell phone chirped. "Tony, what a pleasant surprise."

"Just wanted to thank you for that lawyer," Tony said. "He says everything is pretty much done, so it won't take too long to tie up the loose ends."

"That's great," Jade said. "I'm so glad you called. I've been thinking about the house. Do you have any idea what you might ask for it?"

"Well, no," Tony said. "But I could get hold of a real estate person, talk with my brother and sister, and see what we can come up with. I can probably let you know in the next couple of days, if that's all right."

"That'd be fine. Of course I haven't checked into financing yet," Jade added quickly. "I just wanted to let you know, before you actually list it, that I'm interested."

"Good to know. Thanks. I'll be in touch."

As soon as they clicked off, Jade's mind started to race. *Now you've done it. Now what are you going to do?* It took a couple of heartbeats to shift from right brain to left brain. Of course, area comps. She needed to come up with her own estimate as to what the house was worth.

Within the hour (thanks to a co-worker's realtor wife), she was holding a fax of the area's current listings, pendings, and solds. Not that it did a lot of good. The area was so diverse; numbers were all over the board. Year built, square footage, architectural style, building materials. What made the neighborhood charming also made it a pricing nightmare. She would have to go by each address to find out if any was truly a viable comparison. A glance at the wall clock told her it was quitting time and time to do property drive-bys before rush hour gridlock.

By 6:30, Jade was propped in front of her home's computer screen, comparing her comp sheet with the MLS screen and managing an occasional bite of her Chinese combo plate from Lucky's. There was one possibility, but the place had been totally restored prior to sale. She grabbed a piece of paper, pencil and calculator. As she mentally did a walk-through of the Atwood property, she jotted down areas that needed immediate attention, desirable decorative and cosmetic ideas, and associated costs for each. She stared at the total, which was quite a bit more than she had hoped. And who knew what lurked beneath the visible. Add another 10% minimum for unforeseen costs. Should it be more? Her stomach turned. Rehabs are nothing but a crap shoot, Jade thought, and her financials didn't look like she was in much of a position to roll the dice. She was just about ready to call Tony and renege on the idea when a thought popped into her mind. Maybe there was a way ... .

---

*Go to the Appendix for the articles entitled **Getting From At-Home to On-the-Job** and **Sleepwalking Through Your Workday?** Visit starrcochran.com for two worksheets entitled **Sample Career Action Plan** and **Career Gap Analysis.***

Fourteen

For Rita lunch at Lori's office had been a nice break from the pressure which had become a part of her life since Cliff died – their personal finances in turmoil, her husband's beloved business in trouble. Rita's heart thumped loud in her ears; she felt SterTechCo's future fading by the hour. Two months was not much time. Surely Cliff knew. He had to have known. Facing his company's imminent demise was probably too much for his already weakened heart. Years of worry, she thought. Yet he never let on. He never shared. Perhaps things would have turned out differently.

Christine, Brian, and Glen interrupted her thoughts. "Ready for us?" Christine asked as the trio walked into Rita's office.

"Yes," Rita answered, rising from the couch. "I was just thinking about your father."

"I know. It's still not real," Christine added.

Rita motioned to the sitting area. Brian and Christine took opposite ends of the upholstered sofa located between two leather wingbacks, which flanked the couch; Glen and Rita seated themselves in the chairs. Rita picked up a legal pad and pen and took a deep breath. "Brian, what did you learn from your meeting with Michelle?

Brian positioned himself on the edge of his seat, arms resting on his thighs. "Really nothing we didn't already know," he answered. "Expenses are on automatic pilot, and unfortunately, it doesn't look like there's much leeway."

"*Anywhere* we could trim costs?" Rita asked

He shook his head. "Rent and utilities are constant. Salaries are a big expense, but everyone is critical, especially now."

"Then it sounds like it's a matter of completing the contracts so we get paid," Rita said. Everyone nodded in agreement. "If that's the case, then it's up to Kerry's group, right?"

Glen uncrossed his legs and straightened. "Technically speaking, but as you heard this morning it's a lot more complicated than that. Kerry doesn't have the resources to make significant programming changes."

"It was that way for as long as I was around," Christine jumped in. "The deployment group operates in crisis mode. There's always a deadline looming and always a glitch pushing the deadline out."

Rita felt SterTechCo's impeding doom. Department heads were arguing. Technical challenges were grinding progress to a halt. Even with Glen's help, she was still responsible to pull her own weight. The learning curve was steep. Rita frowned. "If Kerry doesn't have enough people to handle the reworks, then it seems logical to me that Saleem's group should do them. Is there any reason why he couldn't?"

Silence befell the room. "No, but he's not going to like the idea," Christine began. "You heard him – he doesn't believe that's in his job description."

"Maybe it's time to redefine his job description," Rita said. "What do you think, Glen?"

"I think it's the key to getting us out of the situation we're in, but I agree with Christine – I'm not sure he's going to play along."

"What if he doesn't?" Rita asked.

Christine answered. "Dad always thought he was indispensable, so he did whatever it took to appease Saleem, and the rest of us had to suck it up. Frankly, he's been the monkeywrench in the works. If he doesn't like it, I say let him leave."

"Amen to that," Glen piped in.

"Wouldn't that cause a problem?" Rita asked.

"His right-hand person, Damith, could step in," Glen answered. "He's been here long enough; he knows what's going on."

Christine nodded. "Besides that position won't be as critical if we decide to move our primary focus from software development to consulting."

Glen and Rita leaned into the group in tandem; their mouths dropped, and their eyes widened.

"That's the first I've heard of this," Glen said.

"Me, too," Rita chimed in.

Christine assumed an executive posture and spoke to Rita. "Brian and I have been talking since our meeting at Blue Willow. Obviously, SterTechCo's short-term financial issues must be the current focus, but we still believe that the company's long-term sustainability rests in its ability to meet clients' expanding technology needs, which is in the area of consulting." Christine turned her attention to Glen. "You know as well as anybody that the software has been sold to just about everybody who can use it. Without a new direction we'll be confined to maintenance contracts, which will hardly keep the lights on."

The leather chair groaned as Glen shifted his weight and cleared his throat. "Yeah, but, making a switch like that is a subject we need to discuss somewhere down the road – not today."

"I wouldn't have even brought it up if we hadn't been talking about Saleem," Christine said.

Rita took the floor. "I agree with both of you. If clients for the software are diminishing, then SterTechCo needs to look for new markets, but let's just get through the next couple of months." A nod came from each person in the group. "Getting back to Saleem, I'd like to talk with him."

"Sure," Glen said. "Maybe you'll have better luck than I've had."

"Glen," Rita continued. "If you would meet with Kerry today and get timelines for current projects, we could get together first thing tomorrow and invite anybody you feel is necessary for a strategic planning session. I'll ask Saleem to join us." She turned to Christine and Brian. "You're welcome to sit in on any and all meetings. I'll leave that up to you and your schedules."

"Thank you," Christine answered and glanced at her brother. "I think I speak for both of us that you and Glen can take it from here. Let us know if there's anything we can do."

Everyone nodded, and Rita hurried out the door.

Saleem was hunched over his keyboard, frowning at the screen. "Do you have a minute?" Rita asked as she rapped lightly on the open door.

"Yes. Please come in." He motioned to the empty chair along the wall and swiveled around to face her.

"How's it going?" Rita asked.

"As usual. Too much work, not enough time."

Rita took a deep breath. "In general terms I'm familiar with what goes on here and who's responsible for what, but I'd like for you to describe your position in the company ... what you do, how your work fits in the big picture."

He leaned back in his chair and crossed his arms. "Very simple. My job is to develop new versions of the software. As changes are made, they are passed on to Kerry's group for implementation."

"Sounds pretty straightforward. So, why is there friction between the two of you?"

"She thinks that Damith and I should fix coding glitches in previous versions."

"And you believe that her people should fix them," Rita finished his thought, and he nodded in agreement. "When a new version is completed, isn't it tested?"

"Yes, but small issues come up during implementation that can't be anticipated during development. She wants to throw the problems back in my lap when her programmers can easily reconcile them."

"What do you think can be done to resolve this issue between you and Kerry?"

"Let me do what I was hired to do." He had dug in his heels, and she felt the brush-off.

"As I said in the meeting this morning my focus is on the team effort, so for the time being I'm asking that you put your new development activities on hold and place your focus on working with Kerry on the bugs."

The room fell silent except for the crackle of the hard drive. Saleem leaned further back in his chair until his head rested against the wall. "I see."

Rita read the message loud and clear, but she had to get through to him. Maybe they could get by without him, but she didn't want to find out too late that maybe they couldn't. "Two months isn't a lot of time. Either we meet the deliverable deadlines and get paid, or a new version of the software will be pointless because there will be no SterTechCo." Rita paused, and her tone softened. "You've been here since the beginning. I hope you'll be part of the team to do whatever it takes to assure its future."

Moments ticked by. Saleem maintained his power position. Rita remained steadfast, hardly breathing. Finally Saleem, unfolded his arms and placed his hands on his knees. "Okay, yes, we must do this."

Rita blew out a sigh and rose from her chair. "Good. Thank you. I've called a strategy meeting for nine tomorrow morning in Cliff's, I mean, my office. I'll see you then." The two gave each other a quick nod, and Rita left his office.

Carmen's desk was spotless and her chair snuggled up against the middle drawer – the way she always left her work area at the end of the day, Rita thought as she passed by and into her own office. Luckily, she had closed the blinds before leaving. The glassed office with its western exposure suffered the worst of the desert's sun in late afternoon. Double-paned, UV-filmed windows, window coverings, and air conditioning units doing double time could only reduce the temperature from unbearable to tolerable.

Rita removed her blazer and draped it across the back of Cliff's chair. No more putting it off – it was time to go through the papers on his desk. The first stack contained personnel evaluations for Kerry's group – all good workers, all deserving of a raise, all would have to be put on hold. Contracts ready for signature took up the right side of the desk along with requests for proposals, more deadlines, which she planned to talk about at tomorrow's meeting. A request for additional hardware from Saleem had been placed in the upper corner of the desk almost out of reach; its placement said it all.

Giving way to the day's information overload and emotional chaos, Rita allowed her body to relax into the chair, but it didn't feel right. The fit was wrong. Was the same true about her being at SterTechCo? She shifted and wiggled, but she couldn't find a comfortable spot. And then it hit her – she was never going to be Cliff. She needed to find her own spot, her way of fitting into the company, and it started with a different chair tomorrow.

Fifteen

Lori walked through her front door, leafing through the day's mail. Ah, the Discover bill. The sight always brought a cold sweat, and the weight of this one sent another chill through her body. Of course, it made sense to charge everything on the card to get the cash back, then pay it off every month, but Bob's spending had been rising exponentially in the last couple of months. Lori ripped the envelope open and was examining the charges when the screeching of the garage door brought her attention back to the present.

"Hi, Sweetie," Bob said as he walked through the door and gave her a kiss.

"How was court?" Lori asked.

"Good. But I'm tired." He stretched his neck side-to-side, causing it to make multiple popping sounds. "This working nights and going to court during the day is kicking my butt. How was your day?"

"The girls and I got together for our first working lunch about money. Today it was about cash flow."

"Sounds like loads of fun," Bob said with an eye roll. He pulled the off-duty gun from his waistband and headed toward their bedroom.

"You know how I love to teach," Lori said as she followed him down the hall. "And they're eager to learn. Although right now they probably learned more than they wanted to know, but everybody has to start with what's going on with their own money." She drew a breath. "Speaking of which, the Discover bill came today."

Bob secured his gun on the closet's top shelf, shrugged off the Dockers and button-down shirt, stuffed them in the hamper and slipped on jeans and a T-shirt. The long silence told her this wasn't going to be easy.

"Didn't we just talk about this the other day?" There was a twinge of disgust in his tone.

"Yes, and you agreed to financial date night," Lori said. "It's time to pay the bills."

"There's no getting out of this, huh?" Bob asked. Lori shook her head. "Then let's get it over with."

For the most part, Bob didn't like being a grown-up. He preferred to have fun and leave life's boring tasks and responsibilities to someone else, namely her – the disciplinarian, the one to always say no, the juggler of funds between accounts to cover the monthly bills.

Lori took his hand and all but dragged him into the kitchen. Bob pulled a chair away from the table and positioned himself far back in his seat, putting as much distance as possible between him and the dreaded task without being in the next room. Lori shook off the attitude and retrieved the bills, credit card statements, pay stubs, and checkbook from the pocket organizer that hung on the wall next to the back door, and spread them on the kitchen table. "The end of the month means that the mortgage, car payments and electric are due. Of course we have to pay the child care weekly," she said, stacking current bills into a pile. She opened the checkbook and glanced at the balance. "Did you make any cash withdrawals lately?"

"Oh, yeah," Bob answered, retrieved a small stack of ATM receipts from his wallet, and handed them to Lori.

She leafed through the slips of paper. "Ohmigod, Bob! Where's all this money going?" Lori attempted to squelch her frustration, but Bob went through cash like it had an expiration date.

"Some of those are old. I just hadn't gotten around to giving them to you," Bob attempted to justify.

"Still. There's a lot of cash going out! What have you been buying?"

"Coffee, lunch … sometimes my partner is short. He squares with me eventually," Bob defended.

She wondered if "eventually" ever came.

"I know you have to eat out and take breaks," Lori said. "But this looks like a lot more than just that. Think, Bob, what else have you been spending cash on?"

When the moment of silence finally broke, Bob's voice was barely audible. "Well, I did put a gun on layaway at Murphy's."

"Another gun? For crying out loud, Bob, what do you need with another gun?"

"I knew you were going to go ballistic. That's why I didn't want to tell you." He jumped up, stormed over to the refrigerator, yanked on the handle and pulled out a Pepsi. He stood at the kitchen window and popped the can's top as he stared into the backyard.

"You knew I was going to be upset because you already have a small arsenal in the gun safe," Lori said.

He turned to face her. "They're a great investment. I could sell them any time and make a profit."

The money discussion had all the makings of another argument. Not this time, she thought. Lori bit her tongue and squelched the knee-jerk response to say, *We may just have to see about that.*

"We'll talk about investments in just a minute," Lori said. "Getting back to cash withdrawals … ."

Bob interrupted her. "What about you? Where's *your* cash going?"

"Mostly sodas while I'm doing errands and client lunches," she replied and took a breath. "Frankly, I think we could both use some discipline in this area." She entered the additional cash withdrawals into the check register. "Come look how much cash we've taken out just in the last month."

Bob walked over to the table and scooted his chair in close. Lori pointed to the entries. "This is a boatload of money going out, and we need to get a handle on this. How about we each get so much a week for pocket money? We can spend it however we want, no questions asked, but when it's gone, it's gone."

"You're kidding, right? Like an allowance?" He gave a snicker.

"Bob, this can make a big difference. Let's give it a try for a couple of weeks and see what happens."

Moments ticked by. After years of arguing about money, Lori could read her husband's mind. He was trying to figure a way out of this.

"I got nothing," Bob admitted, raising his hands slightly, then letting them fall back on his knees.

"Wow. Okay." The quick surrender surprised her. Was it another brush off, or dare she think she was getting through to him? Time would tell. When it came to money matters, Bob's MO was to say what she wanted to hear, then do what he wanted to do. Even if he went along with the weekly allowance idea, they still had a long way to go.

Lori entered automatic deposits from their jobs into the register, wrote checks for current expenses, recorded those entries, and clicked calculator keys. She presented the bottom line to Bob. "This is what we have left until we get paid again. And here is the Discover bill that is due out of the next pay period along with the rest of the utilities."

His eyes scanned the entries and he shook his head. "I didn't think I charged quite that much."

"That's exactly what I'm talking about," Lori said. "There's cash flying out of the checking account for we don't know what, and we charge like someone else is going to pay the bill. Let's look at what we're buying." She presented the bill in such a way so that Bob could review it. "Toys for the kids that they play with for a couple of weeks? Toys for us that collect dust in the garage? I want our money to do more than that."

Seconds of silence ticked into a minute. "I didn't know you were that unhappy," Bob said, closing the distance between them and laying his hand on top of hers.

Lori looked into his eyes. "It's not that I'm unhappy exactly; it's just that sometimes I think we're leading separate lives."

"I would say more like we're just busy doing what we do," Bob said. "We work at our jobs, then work around the house. We share the kids' activities. And until the other day I thought you were fine with handling the family's finances."

"Handling" was hardly the word Lori would have chosen to describe her interaction with their money – more like a scavenger hunt with sheer panic thrown in on a semi-monthly basis. "All I've been doing is moving money around," Lori said. "It's time for some financial planning. It's time to talk about what's important to us."

"What's important to me right now is the other part of our deal," Bob said as he reached around her waist and pulled her toward him. "I remember something about a date."

She pushed him away. "Hold on. I'm not done with the financial part yet."

Bob blew a loud sigh out his nose. "What else do you want to talk about?"

"Come on now. This is the fun part."

"It's about time."

"If we could work out a budget that we can both live with," Lori started, "there will be money to save and invest."

"Oh, yeah. That sounds like fun," Bob retorted.

"It is. First, we need to put some money away into a savings account as an emergency fund."

"And that is fun, how?" Bob interrupted.

"We could make a game of it – see how fast we could put away, let's say, $1,000." Not that $1,000 was enough for an emergency fund, but it was a start, better than nothing.

"Okay. I'm up for the challenge," Bob said. "So, what do I win if I do it, let's say, in 30 days?"

"You name it," Lori said.

"Oh, baby, you have no idea what you're letting yourself in for," he said with a smirk.

"I'm willing to take my chances." She smiled.

"Then let the games begin." Bob winked.

Lori blushed. The prize was always the same. "Ah, I have a couple of ideas to get you started."

"You want me to win?" The mood was playful.

"Why wouldn't I? I figure it's a win, win."

His right brow inched up slightly. "What do you have in mind?"

Let's see how serious he really is, Lori thought. "How about it if the whole family goes through the house and sees how much stuff we can come up with that we can sell on *craigslist*."

"Wait a minute. You talked about our cash withdrawals, not getting rid of stuff. I like our stuff."

"Game too tough for you already?" Lori pushed to keep the discussion light and to appeal to his competitive spirit.

"Not at all."

"Good," Lori said. "We've agreed to sell some items we don't use any more and to come up with an allowance amount, and I want us to also agree that neither of us will charge anything except for groceries and gas without talking with the other."

"Wait a minute." Bob's eyes bugged out in utter disbelief. "You're taking away my money *and* my credit cards?"

Asking Bob to give up charging was like asking him not to breathe. The credit card was his addiction – it was always there for him; it bought stuff that made him feel good – which made the request the hardest sell. But if she couldn't convince him to kick the habit, there was little hope of getting their financial life on track.

"Think of it as getting to your goal that much faster." The proposal was met with the *is-that-all-you-got* look. Lori cocked her head and spoke softly. "What's been going on with you lately?"

"Are you trying to change the subject?"

"No. It's just that we haven't been talking much lately, and all the spending . . ." Lori's voice trailed off.

Bob shrugged. "No big mystery. I surf the net; I find interesting things. I'm working nights; you and the girls aren't around when I'm up. It's something to do."

"I've got an idea," Lori said, looking into her husband's eyes. "You research everything before you buy it, right?" Bob nodded. "You can do the same thing with investments. Only instead of purchases gathering dust and decreasing in value, investments can increase in value and produce income."

"Hmm." Bob stared at the corner of the ceiling and stroked his chin. "I do like to shop for a good deal."

"I can show you how to evaluate stocks and mutual funds, and we can work on the choices together."

"Okay, that sounds interesting."

"So, we're in agreement about the charging issue?" Lori asked with her fingers crossed.

"How did we get back on that again?" Bob asked, his brows furrowed.

The atmosphere began to cool. She had to think fast before it made it to cold. Talk his language. "You've told me that when you're going into a building after a suspect, you plan your approach, contain the subject by covering the exits, then strike quickly as a team to make a safe capture, right?"

His head bounced in agreement.

"What I'm talking about is how we're going to capture money."

A quizzical look crossed his face.

"The first step in my plan is selling some of our stuff. Then we contain our money in a savings account by covering its possible escape routes – purchases made through credit cards and cash – and work together to keep it safely in custody."

Bob appeared to process the comparison and slowly began to nod. "Okay, I get it."

"Good. It'll be fun. You'll see."

He glanced at his watch and a smile stretched across his face. Grabbing Lori's chair, he closed the gap between them. "Speaking of fun, it seems like we have a little time before dinner. Can I show you *my* idea of fun?"

"Wait, wait, wait," Lori begged him off. "I haven't told you what I want if *I* win our little wager."

His eyebrow inched a notch.

"You have to sell one of your guns." Lori waited with trepidation, hoping he'd take the bait.

He frowned.

"My choice."

He grunted. "Like that's going to happen, babe. Okay. Now let's see, where was I?"

Suddenly, the back door flew open, and Angela and Taunya rushed into the house, yelling, "Mommy, Daddy."

The coach followed them into the room just as Lori and Bob got up to catch the kids in their arms.

"How was soccer?" Lori asked the group.

"They're amazing," Coach said. "The way they move the ball across the field is pure magic. And they have such fun doing it."

Bob leaned into Lori and whispered. "At least *someone* was having a good time this afternoon."

Lori nudged her husband. "Come on, girls. Let's get you cleaned up for dinner. And thanks for bringing them home, Coach."

"No problem."

Lori scooted Angela and Taunya toward the hall bath and put herself on automatic pilot while she mulled over the afternoon's discussion. Had she gotten through to Bob? Maybe. He loved a good game. Maybe not. Behavior patterns ran deep, and his attention span ran short. One thing for sure – she didn't have a lot time.

---

*Go to the Appendix for the article **How to Avoid Dueling Dialogue About Money**.*

Sixteen

Rita dropped into a swivel chair in Lori's conference room and allowed papers to spill onto the table. "I'm exhausted. I have a migraine, and it's only noon. I don't know how Cliff did it all those years."

Lori wiped the glass tabletop with Windex. "I hear ya. I suggested we purge the house and garage of unwanted stuff, and you wouldn't believe the ordeal that was. Three hours of arguing netted two items. This project could take until I'm eligible for Social Security." She leaned over to inspect for fingerprints. "So, how's it going at SterTechCo?"

"Oh, I don't know. I'm still trying to figure that out. The one thing I have learned is that technology is fickle. One minute it's your friend, the next it's your living hell."

There was a commotion coming from the front door. Lori and Rita rushed to the office entrance and found Marla wedged against the door, struggling to balance an oversized portfolio folder under her left arm, a lunch bag in her right hand, and a shoulder bag sliding toward her wrist. In a second Jade trotted up behind her and grabbed the door.

"Can I take something for you?" Jade asked.

"I think I got it," Marla panted. "But I'd appreciate it if you'd make sure I don't destroy anything on the way to the conference room." She followed Jade down the hall and to the left through the door. Once to their destination, Marla allowed the assorted totes to gently fall to the carpet. "I had this great idea," she announced. "I'm so excited. I've been working on it all weekend."

"Tell us. Tell us," Lori said, "before you burst."

The group gathered around the table and started to open soda cans and plastic containers while Marla pulled various-sized sheets of paper out of her purse and the large black portfolio. Her voice was panting with excitement; her gestures were animated with enthusiasm. "After our last meeting I knew I needed to start bringing in some money, so I went through the classifieds, which was very discouraging. Nothing fit. I had the wrong degree, not enough degrees, no experience." She took a deep breath, and the cadence of her speech increased to just short of the disclaimer trailer on a televised special offer. "Well, anyway, the kids asked me to color with them, and of course I had HGTV on. As part of the finishing touches, the designers demonstrated how you could paint a design on a piece of wood and hang it on the wall to bring the room together. All of a sudden it came to me! I could create drawings on canvas that people can paint whatever colors they want." Marla's eyes sparkled, and her face glowed. "The sketches are very simple. Here, look." She laid three sheets of canvas paper on the table. "As you can see in this particular trio of vased flowers, each grouping is different, but the background design carries over." Her friends stood and examined the drawings and nodded. "To begin with, I thought I'd offer simple contemporary designs, flowers and something with a kitchen theme. You could buy them on canvas or on tracing paper if you wanted to transfer the design to another surface or even download them to a printer."

"Very cool," Lori said. "And also relatively inexpensive to get started. Were you planning on selling it as a kit?"

"That was the idea," Marla answered. "It will include the sketches, which I think I can get reproduced at a minimal cost, instructions, and paint and brushes, which are going to be the most expensive components of the project, so I'm still researching online to find the best deal."

"You're planning to sell your product on the Internet?" Rita asked.

Marla was so excited she could hardly control herself. "Yes. I was going to use *craigslist* to start with because it doesn't charge selling fees, but I found out it's more of a local digital 'classifieds' site, and I want to sell nationally, maybe even internationally. So I'll probably use *eBay*."

"Have you come up with a name for the business yet?" Jade asked.

"Right now it's 'DIY' or 'Do-It-Yourself Wall Art.'"

"Catchy," Rita said.

The group took their seats again.

Lori piped in. "Did you talk to Ned about the business part yet? Tax ID number, sales tax number, coordinating supplies and that sort of thing?"

"I haven't said anything to Ned. I wanted to make sure all of this was doable before I talked with him."

Jade picked up one of the paper canvases and smiled as she studied the still lifes. "These are pretty good. And I thought I was the creative one in the group."

Marla beamed. "Thanks."

"Not to put a damper on all this," Jade continued. "But do you really think you can make it a business? I mean, it's a cute idea, but in order for it to be a business, you have to make a profit. Have you figured that out yet?"

"No. Honestly, I just came up with the idea. And at this point I'm not sure if I *can* make any money, which is why I was going to ask Lori if she'd help with the numbers part of it."

"I'd be happy to," Lori said. "We could get together tomorrow."

"Perfect. Let's look at your appointment book before I go."

"Getting back to the product itself for a moment, have you thought about *critical success*?" Lori asked.

"What?" Marla's brow furrowed.

"Are you prepared for the chance that your products will be an overnight success?" Lori asked Marla.

"You mean, what am I going to do if I get a lot of orders at one time?" Lori nodded. "Not really. In the beginning I figured I would use tracing paper and draw them myself."

Lori had seen this phenomenon occur with several clients – a good idea gets thwarted due to poor planning. "What if this is the next best idea since pet rocks? That's a lot of tracing. Have you checked into having your designs printed by a local company?"

Marla scribbled on the yellow pad in front of her. "It's on my 'to do' list. Thanks."

"That's exciting stuff," Lori said. "Anybody else have anything for Marla?" The friends checked with one another, and when the question was met with silence, Lori continued. "Okay, keep us posted on your progress, and let us know if we can do anything to help."

Lori checked her watch. "Look at the time. I'm afraid I've got a client coming in a couple of minutes. Can everybody meet back here the day after tomorrow? We need to cover the Balance Sheet and hear about everybody else's money-making ideas." A collective nod made its way around the table as the women gathered their papers and lunch paraphernalia. "Great! Sorry about this. Oh, Marla, let's look at my appointment book."

Hugs were exchanged as everybody got to their feet and made their way toward the reception area. As soon as the last goodbye had been spoken, Lori's next client arrived.

*Go to the Appendix for the article **So You Have An Idea –
Now What?***

Seventeen

Springs in Tucson had been getting shorter, but this year the season had been skipped altogether. By the time Marla dropped the kids off at school, the temperature was well on its way toward the forecasted high of 100 degrees, and unfortunately, there wasn't going to be the traditional summer reprieve in San Diego this year. At this point the budget didn't have enough wiggle room for a day at the zoo much less a vacation. She cursed the heat, cranked up the car's air conditioning, and pulled out into traffic toward Lori's office.

"Thanks so much for agreeing to help me with this," Marla said as she hugged her friend hello.

"I'm very excited about your project." Lori steered her toward her office. "I'm happy to do whatever I can."

Lori slid onto her plum leather, executive chair, and Marla pulled a chair in close to the desk.

"How about telling me what you've done so far," Lori asked.

Marla referred to the notes in front of her. "I researched the idea, and I haven't been able to find anything quite like it. Paint-by-number projects have been around a long time, but my designs are simpler with broader strokes and with colors picked by the customer." Lori nodded.

"I checked to make sure that the domain name of my product was available and registered it."

"Have you nailed down prices for all your supplies?" Lori asked.

Marla presented an itemized list. "At first I thought I'd use canvas paper, but it was going to be too expensive to print on that. I found that if I used a heavy acrylic paper, the drawings could be copied, and the cost would be minimal." She continued as Lori examined the numbers. "I'm pretty happy with the prices for the other supplies, but I'm still looking for even less expensive options without sacrificing quality. I want to offer a good product at a reasonable cost."

"Have you thought about who your customer is?" Lori asked.

"Hmm." Marla contemplated the question. "I would say mostly women like me – at-home moms who enjoy decorating and want something unique and inexpensive."

"Given that, how would you market your product?"

Marla pulled out another piece of paper and handed it to Lori. "I jotted down some ideas. Craft stores, art supply stores. I'm wading through a ton of websites that sell new products, and I've contacted HGTV about advertising on their site. Haven't heard back from them yet."

"Wow! You've been busy!" Lori said. "Usually my clients aren't this prepared. That's great!" She thought a minute before proceeding. "Let's see. What about your own website?"

"Oh, yes!" Marla smiled and presented a sketched web design. "My friend, Vivian, roughed out a few suggestions for the layout and essential links. What do you think?"

Lori scanned the drawing. "It looks great! Can't wait to see how the finished website turns out!" She studied the diagram a few more minutes. "What payment system are you going to use?"

"Vivian told me that Pay Pal is secure with minimum fees. Sounded like a good place to start."

"You'll need a company bank account," Lori said, "which is where I think I come in, right?"

"Yes, the business part of the business," Marla agreed.

"Here is the checklist I give to everybody starting up a new business," Lori said, handing one to Marla. Lori couldn't be happier that

Marla was in her office seeking professional advice to set up her business. Most of the time Lori counseled clients and had to make referrals to attorneys after the parties had made critical decisions based on misinformation, after the business had gone south, or after partners had quit talking to each other. "One of the first things you need to decide is how you want your business to be taxed – sole proprietorship, partnership, or corporation. Do you have plans to have a partner at this point?"

"No. Do I need one? And wouldn't it be simpler if I didn't have one? Does Ned count as a partner?"

"For the most part I think you could run the business on your own at this point," Lori said. "The only caveat would be the accounting aspect. In addition to regular bookkeeping issues such as income and operating expenses, there are such things as inventory and sales tax reports to keep current. Again, I think with some guidance you could handle the bookkeeping part as well. Do you think Ned would help you get started?"

The last thing she wanted to do at this point was ask Ned for help. Between the stress of tax season and their financial woes, she was in no mood to deal with his attitude. Besides, this was her baby, and it was important for her to figure this out on her own. She knew him all too well – as soon as she mentioned her idea, he'd want to take over, and it wouldn't be hers anymore. "I would prefer to leave him out of this for now. What would you suggest?"

Lori thought about this for a moment. There was no money in the budget for an accountant, and the level of expertise Marla needed was beyond Lori's. "Can you think of anybody who has some bookkeeping or accounting background? Maybe someone from the kids' school?"

Marla tapped her lips with her index finger. "Now that you mention it, Rachel's mom is a retired accountant. I could ask her if she'd be able to help me out.

"That's a great idea. Let me know."

"Okay. I will," Marla replied. "Getting back to taxing the business … if it's just me, what type of business should I have?"

"There are two ways you could go: sole proprietorship or corporation," Lori answered. "With the sole proprietorship there's no paperwork involved. Pretty much you just say you're in business, and that's it. Business income and expenses are reported on your personal tax return."

"I'm for simple," Marla said. "The corporation route sounds complicated. I don't think I need that, do you?"

Lori shook her head. "Not to start off. The reasons to incorporate are liability, taxes, and business continuum. Given your product I don't see a liability issue – meaning that I can't think of a reason for anybody to sue you. Secondly, there are tax benefits to incorporating. However, in the beginning when profitability is generally low, the business should have a minimal impact on your tax situation. Eventually, you can check with Ned on that. And as far as the business continuing should something happen to you, that becomes more of a concern once the business gets off the ground." Lori paused to let the information sink in.

A frown settled on Marla's face. "I've heard a lot about LLCs. Should I do one of those?"

"You're a glutton for punishment, aren't you?" Lori said.

"This is great stuff, really."

"Okay, you asked for it." Lori took a breath. "LLCs or Limited Liability Companies are legal entities created and regulated by state law. They have the same limited liability characteristics as corporations, but are generally treated like partnerships for income tax purposes."

"So since I don't have a partner, I can't do an LLC, right?" Marla asked.

"This is where it gets a little confusing. Actually, you can form an LLC and choose to be treated as a corporation or sole proprietor for tax purposes."

"But you don't think I need an LLC." The comment was more a question than a statement. Gathering information on the Internet, comparing supply prices, drawing and painting the templates had all been fun; this business stuff, not so much. In fact, her brain was beginning to ache.

"When starting up a business, I'm all for starting simple and adding layers of complication as needed. Let's see how things go."

"Sounds good to me. What do I need to do to get started?" Marla asked.

"An Arizona sales tax number, a city sales tax number, and you have to register your business name with the state."

All this information was beginning to take its toll. Who would have thought wanting to sell some do-it-yourself artwork would involve so much?

Lori interrupted Marla's mental sidebar. "Are you ready to get started?"

"Absolutely!"

Lori stood. "Let's go downtown and register your company's name, and then we can come back here and apply for the sales tax numbers. Sound like a plan?"

Marla nodded enthusiastically, and the two headed out the door.

~

Rita woke up on a bit of a management high. The previous day's strategic planning meeting had gone well. Everybody agreed to work together; deadlines looked attainable. They were far from being out of the woods, but she was hopeful.

Kerry bumped into Rita as she stepped off the elevator at Ster-TechCo. "I just came from your office." Kerry spoke in a whisper as they walked side-by-side down the hall toward Rita's office. "I got a call from Howard this morning. He said you told him we were going to make their project deadline two weeks from Friday."

Rita swallowed hard. "Based on our discussion yesterday I thought that's where we were with that project." She dumped her purse and briefcase on the couch in her office and deposited herself behind the executive desk.

"We've got to have a date to shoot for, but it's always a moving target," Kerry explained. "Since I got off the phone with Howard, their system crashed – a result of a new bug in the software. I don't know how long it's going to take to fix it."

"The completion of this project means the biggest payout to us."

Rita powered up her computer. "It's got to be our number one priority."

"It's your call." Kerry shrugged. "But it means I have to pull people off of other projects. What do you want me to tell our other clients?" Her cell phone chirped. She looked at the display, held her index finger up to Rita, listened to the caller for a moment and said, "Great. Shut everything down. I'll be right there." Kerry clicked off and loosened her grip on the phone. "The AC unit for the servers is not working. I'll call building maintenance. While they fix that problem, maybe we'll be able to figure out this new bug."

Rita once again swallowed hard. "Do you want me to call Howard?"

"Yes, thank you. I'll give him a call as soon as I know something about this latest issue," Kerry said, walking backward until she reached the door, then turning to exit.

Self-doubt and frustration shoved Rita back in her chair. *What was I thinking? Maybe I should turn the reins over to Glen. What do I know about running a company? I know even less about technology. What good am I?*

The desk clock ticked. The task wasn't going to get any easier. Rita blew out a sigh, straightened her back, picked up the receiver, and dialed Howard.

~

It was 5:30 p.m. when Rita got home. She dropped her purse and keys on the kitchen counter and kicked off her four-inch Stuart Weitzman pumps. The cooling system was back on.

Howard had understood but was not happy. Everybody was still working on the latest technological bug challenge. Overall, the work day ended up more behind than when it had started.

She shuffled through the pile of mail. Mostly bills and no insurance check. Concern was growing into panic as due dates for personal bills approached and project deadlines were pushed back. Her leave without pay from the television station weighed heavily on Rita. The salary paled in comparison to Cliff's, but at least it was something. The twisting in the pit of her stomach wrenched tighter. Mental note: call insurance company again tomorrow.

More out of habit than hunger, Rita padded her way to the kitchen, yanked on the door handle of the side-by-side, and surveyed the refrigerator's contents. Milk, cheese, lettuce, a few potatoes. Obviously grocery shopping hadn't been high on her priority list lately. She closed the door and walked over to the wall phone to call Lori, who answered after the first ring.

"Do you have any plans for dinner tonight?" she asked Lori.

"I was just thinking about what to do about that. Bob's working, so it's me and the girls. Did you want to come over?"

"Would you mind?" Rita asked. "I've had one of those days, and I don't feel like being alone."

"You're always welcome. See you in a couple minutes."

They clicked off.

The thought of not having to stare at the walls until bedtime gave Rita a burst of energy. She hurried to the bedroom, shimmied out of her skirt, zippered a pair of pink Capri pants and slipped on color-coordinated sandals. Within minutes she was in the car and on her way to her friend's house.

"Boy, that was fast," Lori said as she opened the door.

"Thanks so much for letting me come over." Rita sucked in a deep breath and followed Lori into the kitchen. "Aw, spaghetti. That's just what I need ... comfort food."

"I say, when in doubt, make spaghetti. Have a seat while I get the water started." Lori pulled a big pot from cupboard, filled it two-thirds full, put it on the stove, and switched the burner to high.

Lori took a seat next to Rita at the kitchen table. "Rough day, huh?"

Rita shook her head. "Just when I think I've got a handle on things, something blows up in my face." Lori nodded, and Rita continued. "I had to call our biggest client today and take back my promise on the date we are going to finish his project. Not only are we probably not going to make that deadline, I'm not sure we're going to make any of them."

"So the projects haven't been prioritized?"

"Yesterday that didn't appear to be necessary," Rita said. "Now it may be our only chance."

Lori went to the stove and checked the water. Not time for the pasta, so she returned to her seat at the table. "Any idea which one should take precedence?"

"I thought it should be the largest one, but then Kerry reminded me that of course the other projects would have to be put on hold." Rita played with the ceramic penguin salt and pepper shakers on the table. "Maybe Brian and Christine are right – I have the best intentions but the wrong skill set. Maybe I should step aside and let Glen run solo."

"You're out of your comfort zone. It's normal to feel a little overwhelmed," Lori assured.

"I could go back to reporting, make adjustments in my lifestyle and learn to live on my salary."

"Yes, you could do that," Lori said. "But what happened to wanting to save the company?"

Rita thought about the question a moment. "If Cliff couldn't do it, what makes me think I can?"

"Oh, I don't know – fresh eyes, new energy, new synergy," Lori replied. "You said it yourself, according to the kids, Cliff was stuck, meaning SterTechCo was stuck. It sounds like the company needs some shaking up, and who better to do that than you, looking at everything from a different perspective."

"You really think so?"

"Not only that," Lori said, "but women bring a sense of relationship-building to the table. In the short time you've been there, you got Glen to agree to work with you as a team and Saleem to join Kerry's group to get the projects done."

"Both of which are teetering on the edge of collapse," Rita interjected. "One sign of weakness, and either could bail."

"As a reporter you've been in situations where people didn't want to talk to you, didn't want to answer your questions. And yet you got the story. You established a relationship with them, earned their trust, and they opened up to you. The situation at SterTechCo is a little different, yet very much the same. It's still about relationships and trust."

A shriek of laughter from Angela and Taunya in the family room made the two friends look in that direction. Four sets of eyes followed the cartoon characters as they skipped along the bottom of the plasma screen to the beat of a sing-along. When a commercial for the latest transformer robot began to roll, the girls went back to dressing their dolls, and Lori and Rita resumed their conversation.

"If anybody can keep them on board, Rita, it's you."

"I've never had so much at stake. As a reporter I always had a shot at another story. I won't have a second chance to save SterTechCo."

"You won't need one," Lori said.

"Thanks for the pep talk."

"You're welcome." A sizzle from the stove caused Lori to dash to the boiling water which had begun to spill over the pot. "Angela, Taunya," she called as she dumped the package of angel hair pasta into the pot. "Wash your hands. It's almost dinner."

The heaviness of the spaghetti and the weight of the day made it difficult for Rita to keep her eyes open on the drive home, but the familiarity of the road allowed her to steer on automatic pilot, and within minutes she was pulling into her garage. An echo resounded through the large, dark kitchen when the door closed behind her. She flipped the light switch, then immediately turned it off. She didn't need the light to show her the way to the bedroom or to remind her she was alone. She needed the comfort of darkness and the familiarity of her bed. For tomorrow there would be plenty of light and unknowns to deal with.

*Go to the Appendix for the **Checklist for Starting A New Business** and **Business Entity Comparison**.*

Eighteen

Jade, Rita and Marla each retrieved their papers and lunches from purses and satchels while Lori tacked up large sheets of paper and addressed the group. "I'm glad today worked out for everybody. Who'd like to share what they learned about their net worth?"

"I'll go." Jade raised her hand and was given the go-ahead nod. She took a deep breath. "You'd think with my income that I'd have something to show for it, but as it turns out, I have little or no net worth. Between the remodeling projects and my inability to tell myself 'no' to anything, the credit card balances offset most of my home equity. My only other asset worth talking about is my retirement plan at work, and that's pitiful. I haven't put much in it, and it hasn't done much. I guess mostly because I don't know what I'm doing in that area." The reality of her financial situation had been sobering. She made good money and had little to show for it.

"I don't know about anybody else, but I'm surprised," Marla said. "It seemed like you always had it all together financially. A house, good-paying job, retirement plan."

"Outward appearances have little to do with anything. Look at us, for example." Lori pinned up her Balance Sheet which had been reproduced on a large Post-It. "On the asset side here on the left, I subtotaled each of the categories: cash and savings, investment assets, retirement assets and non-income earning assets." She pointed to each total as she went down the column. "Do you see anything missing from this list?"

There was a collective frown from the group.

"We have no savings," Lori answered. "We should have at least three months of living expenses easily accessible ... so we don't have to rely on credit cards to make ends meet."

"We don't have anything in savings either," Marla said with a look of disgust. "Being an accountant, you'd think he'd know better."

"And he probably *does* know better on an intellectual level," Lori said in a soothing tone. "But finances aren't always just about crunching numbers. If I've learned anything after all these years in this business, money is personal, and decisions are often made emotionally, not logically."

Marla stared at Lori and nodded. "I can see how that could happen."

"Speaking of emotions making the decisions, nobody could be better at that than Bob," Lori said. "He rarely comes across a gismo, gadget or machine that he doesn't fall in love with, and all of them are right here in this section." She waved an index finger at the group of entries on the Balance Sheet entitled "non-income earning assets," which included the personal residence, autos, recreational vehicles, furniture, jewelry, collectibles, etc. "Technically they're assets because they're worth something, but with a few exceptions most of them tend to depreciate or go down in value."

Rita piped in. "Our homes being an exception, right?"

"Exactly," Lori said.

Lori then pointed to the column on the right side of the paper entitled "liabilities." "Here are the mortgage, car loans and credit card balances. Total assets minus total liabilities shows a positive net worth, but ... ." She picked a red Sharpie and circled the non-income earning asset total and the total asset number. "If you compare these two numbers, you'll notice that they are pretty close to the same, which means most of our assets are in the non-income earning category. Needless to say, that's not where we want them to be. The goal here is to have the majority of our assets in every other category, where they can make us money by generating income or going up in value or both," Lori said, making a big red check next to cash and savings, investment assets, and retirement assets.

Everybody circled totals on their statements. Rita stared at her statement which Lori had prepared. The bottom line was nearly as bleak as her friends' although SterTechCo was the big unknown. It could be the asset to pull her out of financial disaster or could be the source of it. The thought twisted and turned in her gut every day, all day. There was no other alternative. Nothing in savings, some in Cliff's IRA, a little in each of their company's retirement plans, house mortgaged to the max. And yes, she had every kind of debt imaginable and her fair share of non-income earning assets. "So how do we change that around?"

"There are a couple of different ways," Lori said to Rita. "One I mentioned to you earlier is that Bob and I are selling some of our stuff on *craigslist*, and we're putting whatever we get into a savings account. That puts real money in a higher category."

Marla's face lit up. "I could do the same thing! I'm going to sell my art projects online anyway. I could sell other stuff, too!"

"I've got tools, building materials and supplies I'm probably not going to use," Jade said. "You know, I didn't think of including those in my Balance Sheet. That's like found money!"

"You're right," Lori said. "And there's more to be had if we examine every aspect of our financial lives ... . What do we buy? Why? What do we need? What do we have? Why? That's the reason for doing these financial statements. They beg us to ask those types of questions."

The questions began to run through Rita's mind, and she was suddenly embarrassed. Her friends only knew the half of it. There were the obvious purchases such as the clothes, shoes and jewelry, but there were those which were not so obvious like massages, dinners at upscale restaurants, and enough Victoria Secret undergarments to last well into her eighties. Reviewing the credit card statements in Cliff's den the other night forced her to come to grips with the ridiculousness of her spending. They never talked about money, their money. It was just always there for whatever, whenever. She had been such a fool. It had to come from somewhere. Cliff must have been under such pressure, she thought. If she had bought less, invested more, put more away, been more financially savvy ... if she had only known.

"What else could we do?" Marla asked, interrupting Rita's thoughts.

"Begin regularly funneling cash into a savings account from our checking accounts," Lori answered.

Marla's face contorted. "How do we do that if we're supposed to be putting everything into paying off our credit cards?"

"The short answer is: it's a balancing act," Lori replied, grabbing a large, blank Post-It sheet and tacking it up on the wall. "We didn't cover this when we talked about cash flow, but it's all connected." Lori began to write percentages in a column. "To strike a healthy financial balance, here's one way to break it down. Our housing expense should be about 35% of our net income, other debt service 10%, transportation 15%, savings 10%, and everything else 30%," she said while printing the category next to each number. "As you can see, this allows for both paying off credit cards and savings." A collective frown indicated there was probably some mental calculating going on. "Getting spending in line on the cash flow side creates more investable dollars for the net worth side."

"Makes sense," Marla said.

"So how did everybody do with their 'cash only' spending last week?" Lori asked.

Each member of the group looked at one another, expecting them to be the first to confess.

"I'll go," Jade finally answered. "I'm so accustomed to using plastic. It felt kinda weird at first. But the biggest thing I noticed about using cash is that each purchase really meant something."

"Go on," Lori said.

"When you use a credit card, it's almost like you're not paying for it. You get the merchandise and a receipt, but you're not seeing the cash physically go out of your wallet or the money deducted from the checkbook every time you purchase something. Does that make sense?"

"You hit the nail right on the head," Lori said. "When we use cash, money becomes real instead of just numbers on a statement. Do you think you spent less last week than other weeks when you charged everything?"

Jade vigorously nodded her head. "Oh, yeah. Definitely."

Lori checked in with Marla and Rita. "Did you have the same experience?"

They both agreed.

"This is great stuff," Jade said. "Getting back to the Balance Sheet, how else can we increase that bottom line?"

"Well, you mentioned your retirement plan earlier," Lori said.

Jade slumped back into her chair and made a dismissive hand gesture. "I'm so frustrated with all of that. I just want to quit putting any more into it. I don't contribute much, and most of the time it looks like it's going more down than up."

"Your employer matches your contributions, right?" Lori asked.

"Three percent."

"Then you should do at least that to take advantage of that free money," Lori explained.

"Okay, but what do I do about it going down?"

"That subject deserves its own lunch meeting, so we'll table that for another time."

"Fair enough." Jade's foot bounced on her crossed leg. "So if the idea is get more assets in the income-producing category, then buying a house to rent out would be good, right?"

Silence fell on the room.

"What house?" Lori asked for the group.

Jade gushed as she began rooting through her purse. "It caught my eye the other day when I was stuck in traffic. The only house in the immediate area that hasn't been converted to office space. I've got pictures." She pulled out her digital camera, turned it on, and dialed to the saved pictures icon. The group gathered around and squinted at the tiny screen while Jade proudly presented several shots of the main house and carriage house from different angles. "It's in good shape, but it needs some work. It's not on the market yet. Part of an estate. I met the son when I was snooping around."

When the picture show was over, the group settled back into their chairs, and some of Jade's words wedged themselves in Rita's mind. Her house. Part of the estate. Would she be able to afford it without Cliff's income? How long could she keep up with the payments, the maintenance? Should she consider selling it? Could she lose her home? She was sad; she was afraid.

"Neat old house all right," Marla said. "Are you moving?"

Jade powered down the camera and put it away. "No. I thought I'd convert it to professional income property."

"So the owner is interested in selling?" Lori asked.

"Yes. Neither he nor his siblings live in the area. We're each doing some research, and I'm checking with a commercial lender to see what I qualify for."

Lori continued in her professional mode. "What have you come up with so far?"

Jade shook her head. "Houses are all so different in that area. I found one place that looks similar, but it's a tough area for comps."

"What about rehab costs?" Lori asked.

Jade sucked in some air. "That's no easy matter either. Old houses are notorious for costly chain-reaction surprises. A friend of my dad's, Harry, is going to take a look at the house for me and let me know what he thinks. He's a home inspector by trade, and he's agreed to do me a favor by giving it the once-over."

"So, let's say you get the commercial loan, how will you pay for the rehab?" Lori asked.

Jade laid her fork on top of the remnants of her salad. "There may be a possibility of increasing my home equity line of credit, or I could use credit cards and pay them off when the rental income starts coming in."

"What if you can't tap your home equity?" Lori continued. The question was met with universal, silent contemplation as everyone avoided Lori's gaze. She wondered if everyone was problem-solving Jade's situation or if it was more personal. They were all tapped out, just in varying degrees. "Looking at your Balance Sheet, I can't see where else you might get the down payment."

"I'm still working on that." Lori's questions had been sobering. Maybe Jade had been blinded by the property's charm, but she wasn't ready to give up quite yet, not until she had gathered all the information.

Lori continued. "Do you know what the vacancy rate is and what you might be able to lease it for?"

"The vacancy rate for the area has gone up slightly over the last few months, but the downtown area is still very desirable for professionals, so I'm not too concerned about finding a tenant. Depending on purchase price and financing, I think I can get close to breaking even," Jade answered.

"Well, it certainly sounds like you found a potential money-making idea." Lori checked the wall clock. "If it's okay with everybody, I'd like to table Rita's and my income-generating ideas until next time because I'd rather get through our Balance Sheets." When the group agreed, Lori nodded toward Marla. "Would you like to talk about yours?"

Marla righted the stack of papers, then frowned at the top sheet. "I'm not sure I did this right. Can I have a negative net worth?"

Lori answered the puzzled faces. "Yes, if you owe more than the value of your assets."

Marla shook her head while staring at her statement. "Then we're a mess. How am I going to get my idea off the ground if I have less than nothing?"

"Luckily, your product doesn't entail a large inventory or huge start-up costs," Lori explained. "I think you could get up and running for a minimal cost."

Marla slumped in her chair. "Maybe I should give up on this business idea and get a job, although I don't know what type of job that would be exactly. I'm not qualified for anything."

"Don't give up yet," Lori said. "Let's see how it goes. Okay?"

Marla mulled the thought over for a moment. "Alright. I suppose I don't have anything to lose at this point."

"True," Lori said. "Rita, do you want to share with Jade and Marla what we found out about your finances?"

Rita straightened her back and focused her attention to her two friends. "Well, Lori discovered Cliff had comingled our personal and SterTechCo finances to the point that it's really one big financial mess. He borrowed from the home equity line and personal credit cards at various times to keep the company afloat; that money has not been repaid. Net worth? There is none. And if we don't get a project or two done very soon, there'll be less than none. The company will be out of business and I'll probably lose everything."

Intellectually, Rita had processed the gravity of her situation, but until those words came out of her mouth, she hadn't fully grasped it emotionally. *She could lose everything.* There was the possibility she'd be back where she started – before Cliff, like the last fifteen years of hard work had never happened.

The seriousness of Rita's situation weighed heavily on the group. If someone they knew could go from the appearance of wealth and prosperity to actual financial ruin, it could happen to any of them.

"Do you think you'll make the deadline?" Lori broke the silence.

Rita shrugged. "It's doable … if everybody continues to get along … if the hardware doesn't crash … if the software doesn't develop a new glitch … if the clients' technology behaves itself. For the 'ifs' beyond my control, I mostly just keep my fingers crossed."

"And for what's *in* your control?" Lori asked.

"Glen and I are working as a team. We've agreed to leave everything financial status quo for the time being, but expenses have already been cut to the bone. Everyone is working overtime to make the deadline. I don't know what else we can do if we don't pull this off."

"Hopefully, you'll never have to find out," Lori said to Rita, then addressed the group. "While each of us are focused on our individual projects and challenges, I think it's important we get together to keep the support and synergy going. What do you think?"

"I totally agree." Jade said.

"Absolutely," Marla piped in.

"Me, too." Rita eyed the clock and rose from her chair. "This has been great, everybody, really. But I've got to get back to work." She stuffed her papers into her purse and snapped the salad container shut. "Thanks for everything. I don't know what I'd do without you guys. See you soon."

The friends followed Rita's lead. Then everyone hugged goodbye.

---

*Go to the Appendix for a blank **Balance Sheet** and the articles: **Increasing Your Net Worth Bottom Line** and **Open Mind for Opportunity**.*

Nineteen

Jade caught herself yawning even though she'd already downed four cups of coffee and the work day was only two hours old. She was about halfway through a long list of changes to her current project when her cell phone chirped.

"Jade. Tony Atwood here."

"Hi, Tony."

"I've talked with my brother and sister and a realtor, and we've come up with a price. I'm in town today. What does your schedule look like?"

She glanced at the wall clock, then at her appointment book. "I could scoot out now, or otherwise, it'd have to be after work."

"It'd probably take me 30 minutes to get downtown. Would that be okay?" he asked.

"How about Starbucks at Campbell and Broadway? Parking's easier there."

"That'll work. I'm on my way."

Jade slipped her phone into the carrying case, took a deep breath and grabbed her purse. She hadn't heard back from the lender, but at least she'd find out if they were even close on a price.

The coffee shop was slow this time of day. The morning's madness of serving the professional commuters their daily caffeine fix was over, which left a few locals relaxing over the daily paper.

Jade stepped up to the counter and ordered. "Vente mocha … wait a minute." She studied the menu for a moment. "Make that a small half decaf, half regular with room for cream."

Jade gave herself a mental high-five. The difference in price between her usual and plain coffee just saved her $3.00. She pulled up to a table and reviewed her offering price and rehab estimates.

"How are ya doing?"

Jade looked up to find Tony tipping his cowboy hat. His gentlemanly manner and old-fashioned gesture made her blush. "Fine, thank you," she replied, getting up and quickly extending her hand to shake his in the hope that he wouldn't notice her reddening cheeks.

"My, that's a lot of paperwork," Tony said as he helped Jade with her chair, sat down on the one next to her and laid his hat off to the side of the table. "Is that all for me?"

"Oh, no. Most are worksheets." Jade shuffled the sheets into a neat stack and selected one in particular to be on top. "You said you came up with a price?"

He pulled out a computer print-out of area comps with a number circled at the bottom and presented it to her. As expected, the number was higher than what she was prepared to offer. "Is that close to what you had in mind?" Tony asked.

"I think we can get there," she said with cautious optimism.

"Well, let me see what you got," Tony said, leaning his elbows on the table and interlacing his fingers.

Jade took a breath. "Okay. These are just some preliminary numbers I threw together based on my brief visit. Of course I would want to get an inspection."

"Of course," he said with a nod.

"Anyway, I began with this number based on the same comps you have," Jade pointed to the number at the top of the column of the top sheet. "As you know, every property is so different in that area, and there's both professional and residential."

Tony nodded.

"Then I added in some basic rehab costs to bring it up to code along with some cosmetic changes, which gives me a purchase price here." Jade tapped a finger by the bottom number.

Tony stared at the figure. "I see."

The air filled with hissing coffee machines, the banging of containers to give up their last caffeinated drops, and customers ordering complicated concoctions. Seconds ticked by while Jade held her breath. She had listened in on enough deals her dad had brokered over the years to know that sometimes buyers thought the value of their home was higher than the market because there was more emotion involved than logic. Jade had her fingers crossed that enough time had passed to tip the scale in favor of logic.

Finally, he looked at her and shrugged. "I guess we didn't think there was that much to be done."

"Oh, it's been very well maintained." Jade's response was quick. "But since it's surrounded by professional office space, I believe the best use of the building is to convert it from residential to professional. And that's where a lot of the costs are."

"By the way, the city changed the zoning for that whole block some years back," Tony said. "Even though we weren't interested, the house was included anyway."

"That's the best news I've heard all day. I'm glad I won't have to go through the expense and hassle of rezoning." Jade paused and sipped her coffee. "But initial costs will be higher going commercial than they would be if it remained a residence. And even though the house is in great shape, just because of its age there may be costs neither one of us are aware of, which is why an inspection is so important."

"Oh, yes," Tony said.

"Are we close enough in price to proceed with an inspection?"

"I think so," Tony assured her.

"Great." She thought a moment. "You know, I might be able to get in touch with this one inspector to take care of that this afternoon. Would you be available to let us in?"

Tony checked his watch, then thought a moment. "I could meet with a friend for lunch and do a little shopping for a while."

"I could call him right now, if you don't mind." When Tony agreed, Jade scrolled through her cell phone directory and pushed the call button. She set up a time with her dad's friend, Harry, and checked with Tony. "How about 2:00?"

"Sounds good to me."

"Thanks for doing this on such short notice," Jade said to Tony.

"Glad to take care of as many errands in town as I can at one time. The driving back and forth is getting a little too much for someone my age."

"We'll find out soon enough whether we can make this deal happen," Jade said. "You know, we're doing this whole thing differently from how it usually goes." A curious look came over Tony's face. "Most of the time the buyer makes a written offer to the seller who either accepts it, rejects it or modifies it. The offer is ordinarily made subject to a satisfactory inspection and loan qualification. We've been rather informal about the process, but it doesn't mean I'm not very serious about the house. We'll learn what we need to know about the structure with the inspection, and I should be hearing about my financing any time. Then we can go from there."

"Sounds like a plan. I'll see you later at the house." Tony placed his hat back on and touched the brim.

~

As soon as Jade had walked through her office door, the land line rang. Caller ID displayed that it was the commercial lender. "Hi, Paul. Thanks for getting back to me so quickly. How does it look?"

"First off, where is the down payment coming from?"

"I was hoping from the equity in my home," Jade replied.

"Studying your Balance Sheet, I figured that. Of course it would depend on the appraisal, but I'm not sure there's enough equity since we typically can only lend up to 80-90% of the appraised value."

"Really?" Jade did not like where this was going. Her home had always been her largest investment and had been there to fund whatever came along – until the historic slide in home values. Even though she had purchased her home pre-boom and stayed in it through the downturn, it didn't mean she had been left unscathed. A huge chunk of her equity had disappeared in a matter of months.

"Even if you could glean the down payment from the home equity," Paul continued, "there are a couple of other criteria which are considered in the total package. You said you were going to occupy an office there, right?"

"Yes, and rent out the other two offices."

"Okay. As an owner-occupied professional space, you'd need to use at least 51% of the space. Also, in order to approve the loan, your annual net business income shown on your tax return would have to be at least 25% above the annual loan payment. Taking the tentative purchase price you gave me and 20% down, which is the minimum you can put down on a commercial loan, and based on the comps, it doesn't look like the area will support the lease amount you'll need to meet the loan criteria."

"There's some more good news." Jade said. "Any suggestions?"

"I would say a lower purchase price is your only option," Paul said. "A larger down payment would be a possibility, but looking at your Balance Sheet, I don't see where that would come from."

Jade gulped and asked a question, already suspecting the answer. "Does that mean you're turning me down?"

"If the building was already rented or ready to rent," Paul explained, "or if you could pick up the property for less, approval *might* be possible. And I emphasize 'might.' We consider the whole package, including the fact you've been a good customer for a long time, but based on these numbers I'd have to say that we can't make the loan."

Jade was devastated. She had never been turned down for a loan. Now what? Tony's asking price was already higher than hers. And *her* number didn't fit into the bank's loan criteria. The inspection was in a matter of hours. Should she call it off?

"Are you still there?" Paul asked.

Jade finally found her voice. "Oh, yes. Sorry. I guess I'm a little surprised, that's all."

"In commercial lending we look at a project more like a business,"

Paul explained. "And as such, cash flows need to be sufficient. When they aren't, we can't make the loan." He paused. "Unfortunately, there isn't as much latitude as there can be on the residential side. And remember, Jade, our lending process is designed to make sure you're not overloaded with loan payments. The last thing I'd want to do is make a loan that would come back later to strain your income."

"I see," she said with a sigh. "Well, thanks for all your help."

"You're welcome," Paul returned. "If there's anything else I can do, please let me know."

"I will." They clicked off.

Jade sank into her chair and crossed her arms. Well, that was that. No financing, no deal. She was embarrassed. She should have gotten prequalified for a loan before talking to Tony about the house. She watched the second hand tick its way around the face of the wall clock. There was still time to call off the inspection. Or ... she could see what Harry came up with. Besides having been her dad's life-long friend, he'd been in the business his whole life. Maybe he'd have an idea or two about how to make this deal work.

~

Tony was leaning against his car in front of the Atwood house when Jade and Harry pulled up.

The men introduced themselves and shook hands. "I've unlocked everything," Tony said. "I'm going to get out of your hair, so take your time and give me a call when you're done."

"Thanks. Will do." Harry nodded and headed back to his truck. He retrieved a ladder, and Jade followed him toward to the house. Dressed in an army-green jumpsuit, Jade kept in step with Harry as he plugged his meter into every outlet, turned the faucets on and off, shined his flashlight through crawl spaces, checked the electrical box, stuck his screwdriver into dry rot, examined the roof, took photos and scribbled a few notes in his spiral pad. The main house looked like it was passing the test. Tony had been right about the carriage house – it was impassable due to an infinite number of boxes. All they could do was shine a light along the roof seam and corners, which did little but disturb a few black widows. The efficiency above the carriage house was unbearably hot, dusty and musty, and in remarkable condition. Two hours later the inspection was done, and so were they – covered in dirt and drenched under their protective clothing.

"So what do you think?" Jade broke the silence.

Harry slid his baseball cap from his forehead, scratched his sweat-soaked hair, then repositioned the hat square on his head. "She's a beauty all right."

Jade nodded and tried to keep her excitement at bay.

"But there's a lot of work to be done to get her up to current code, plus the upgrade to commercial is going to cost a bundle. Then there are always surprises when you start messing with the structure that we can't see at this point. And the carriage house itself is pretty much an unknown because we couldn't get in there to check it out."

"Let's get out of the sun and go through what we know we're looking at," Jade said, motioning toward the back door.

Harry stepped up to the kitchen counter where he had set up his computer and printer, and entered the data from his notepad. Within minutes the printer began to spit out pages at record speed. Harry had been in the business a long time, and when it came to buildings, he had a photographic memory. The report was for the client's benefit; his copy had been imprinted in his brain. "Okay. If you were to convert this house to commercial, you're talking about a lot of money. As an architect, you know that unlike residential rehabs, commercial code says you have to have a city inspector and you have to have a licensed contractor, which adds to the cost."

"You mean I wouldn't be able to do the work myself?"

Harry shook his head. That fact alone would add tens of thousands of dollars to an already staggering budget.

"The code also requires you to beef up the floors to accommodate the additional weight of office equipment like a copier and file cabinets full of paper. Then there's meeting the standards in the bathroom to make it wheelchair accessible, which is going to mean a total redo, and there's handicap accessibility into the building from the outside. Given the slope specs and available area that will mean one heck of a ramp at a hefty price tag. Then there's the parking."

"What do you mean parking? There's plenty of street parking." Each comment brought a loud "ca-*ching*" in her head.

"A commercial building is a commercial building regardless of whether it's new or old, and you've got to have a certain number of spaces according to code. You're used to dealing with new construction, so you may have been somewhat distracted because this is a house," Harry explained. He took a pause. Then, as though plucking a piece of information from his mental data bank, he continued. "Let's see. What else? Oh yeah, you'd have to put in headers above all the doors, and I would venture to say that the inspector would make you totally redo the plumbing and electrical."

Jade was just about ready to thank Harry and write him a check for the inspection when he broke the silence.

"You know, there's another way."

"Really? What's that?"

"If you were to move in and use part of the house as a home office, then you can convert it to commercial after two years or so, and it would be grandfathered in."

"And it wouldn't have to meet all of those commercial requirements you were just telling me about?"

"Yep."

Jade's spirits perked. "So if I was to approach this as a residential project, what costs do you think I'm looking at?"

Harry focused on the kitchen floor and skimmed his mental notes again. "New electrical box for sure." She nodded. "Plumbing, which as you know can be a significant expense, is a big unknown here. According to Tony, his mom redid the plumbing in the place a while back, but the slow water stream is indicating that it may need it again. With low mineral content in the water and not disturbing the pipes, they can last a long time. How long? Who knows? You could be okay for years or bust a pipe tomorrow."

"What's your best guess on the time frame for new plumbing?"

Harry stuck one hand in his pocket and rubbed his chin with the other. "Oh, I would say, count on it in the next few years." He leaned back against the kitchen counter. "Now for some good news. The roof's in good shape. A preventive seal will give you at least five years. No signs of active termites. Most of the wood looks good except for the porch area, which you've already discovered. Windows all work pretty well. You could replace them with double-pane sometime down the road, but they're okay for now."

The printer fell silent. Harry retrieved the stack of papers from the tray, stapled the edge, and handed it to Jade. "You've worked on enough of these types of projects, so I don't have to tell you that there are a lot of unknowns when you start working on houses in the 100-year-old plus range. But if anybody can do it, you can. Your dad would be so proud to see you now."

Suddenly Jade's heart ached at the mention of her father. This would be her first project rehabbing solo start to finish since her dad passed away. The only other house she had purchased was the one she was living in, and he had found it, helped with the negotiations, and even started demolition before he died. This project would be a big risk, but it felt right somehow.

Jade gave him a big hug. "Thanks, Harry. I appreciate your confidence in me. Now I've got to figure out if I can make this deal work for everybody."

"Your dad always said you had a lot of smarts."

"I guess we'll find out soon enough."

---

*Go to the Appendix for the articles: **How to Buy a House – From Dream to Reality**, and **Residential and Commercial Lending**.*

Twenty

Rita stood firmly behind her desk at work and held the phone in a white-knuckle grip. The call to the insurance company about the life insurance check had become as much a part of her routine as a morning cup of coffee. So far the outcome had been the same, and she was growing concerned. If it was in the mail, where was it? If it was lost somewhere and didn't show up for a couple more weeks, how would she pay her bills? There was a rap on the open door. Rita motioned for Glen to come in while she continued talking to the other person on the line. "I don't know what else to say except that I haven't received it yet. Can't you put a stop payment on that check and issue another one?" Glen took a seat on the visitor side of the desk as Rita shook her head, then he listened. "A couple more days? Okay. I'll call back day after tomorrow if I don't receive it by then." She disconnected, dropped into her executive chair and addressed her visitor. "Thanks for coming a little early this morning. I wanted to run my idea by you before our meeting with Kerry and Saleem."

"Shoot."

Rita searched through a stack of papers on the desk, pulled out a sheet, and glanced at it. "I found this project timeline summary on Cliff's desk. It looks like we have the LA project, which is the biggest one, and several smaller ones. If we could deliver on the largest one, the payoff would be enough to give us some breathing room for a couple of months. And if I'm reading this correctly, it looks like we have a pretty good shot at meeting the deadline."

Glen crossed his legs and interlaced his fingers on his lap. "We'd have to check with Kerry, but that sounds about right. Although I have to say, we'd be betting the farm. If we don't make the deadline, we're done."

"I know," Rita said. "When I mentioned to Kerry about focusing on getting the LA project done, she was concerned that the clients on the other projects would get upset. And I'm certainly sensitive to that. But if we put all of our effort into meeting the deadlines on the other projects to the exclusion of LA in the same time frame, I think there is a greater chance of many different kinds of complications because of the uniqueness of the projects. What do you think?"

Glen smiled. "I think you've understood more of what Cliff talked about than I gave you credit for."

Rita returned the smile. The tension across her shoulders eased.

"Sounds like a good strategy." Greg uncrossed his legs. "We'll ask Kerry her thoughts."

"Ask me what?" Kerry entered the office at full speed, followed closely by Saleem. They each pulled up a chair and settled in on either side of Glen.

"Rita and I were discussing the possibility of focusing our resources in meeting the LA deliverable and putting the others on the back burner."

Kerry flipped open her leather portfolio. "I just got an update from my team this morning on all the projects." She reviewed the report. "It could happen, but the move will no doubt piss off the rest of the clients."

"What if most of the team worked on LA and a few people focused on the other projects?" Rita asked.

Again Kerry referred to her timelines and pondered the question for a moment. "Not everybody in my department is familiar with every project, so there would be some time lost getting team members up to speed on LA." She focused on the paper in front of her. "Let's see, I could assign Razmik, Raj, Jack, and Catherine to LA and keep Monette and Barry working on … ." Her voice trailed off as she made notes and drew arrows while the rest of the group watched.

The swirl of names sounded familiar from introductions made at some past company event, but faces were lost in a sea of mostly fresh-out-of-college complexions. "So are we in agreement with this game plan?" Rita asked.

Kerry stopped scribbling and leaned over toward Saleem. "If you would agree to assign Victor and Wayne to the LA team, our chances of meeting the deadline would increase significantly."

Saleem didn't answer right away. Rita sensed some holdover resistance to working with Kerry. He might be on board, but he didn't like it. His gaze focused straight ahead, his lips pressed firmly together, his eyes narrowed minutely, and his crossed foot tapped in midair. "I would say that probably makes sense."

Rita put herself in his shoes. For the short-term his department was getting reassigned, and with that went some of his power. She feared the truce between the two would be brief and the relationship would revert to its tenuous state. There was no time for that. "Good! Glen, since we are temporarily combining two departments … as operations manager, wouldn't it make sense to have you take the lead on this effort?"

Glen cleared his throat. "Yes, it would."

"Everything is riding on this deliverable," Rita said to Kerry. "And that's a lot of pressure on one person. Not that you probably couldn't handle it, but when we can, why not spread the stress?" When Kerry nodded, Rita addressed Glen. "I'm thinking that the next step would be to update the timelines and assign personnel."

"That's right."

"I'd like to sit in on that meeting to get a feel for the process, and then I'll leave you three to do what you do best."

After a collective nod, Kerry spoke. "I have my work assignment spreadsheet in my computer. I'll get that and the projector, and we can meet in the boardroom."

Kerry left, and rest of the group made their way to the conference room.

~

Later that day, Rita took a pitcher of ice tea out of her refrigerator at home, poured a glass, kicked her shoes off, flipped on a few light switches on the way to the living room, and allowed herself a moment of relaxation on the couch. After hours of assigning and adjusting personnel and timelines, she was cautiously optimistic they were going to meet the deadline. Of course there was the matter of getting paid, which could take weeks … or longer, depending on how the client's payment cycle matched up to the completion date. As long as the work was done, and the check was in the mail (so to speak), she was sure she could come up with some way to keep the company going until the actual deposit took place. Speaking of which … .

Rita jumped off the couch, slipped on her shoes and ran to the mailbox. She quickly thumbed through the stack of envelopes. She began to perspire – partially due to the day's lingering heat, but mostly because there was no insurance check again, though there were plenty of bills – electric, pool service, pest control, water. She sulked through the front door, retrieved her glass from the foyer table and collapsed back onto the couch. There was nothing more she could do at SterTechCo for now. Wringing her hands and pacing in her office only chafed her skin and thinned the carpet.

Bits and pieces of the previous day's lunch conversation began to pop in her head. Maybe there was some purging she could do. What did she need with all this stuff anyway? She picked herself up off the couch and began to wander through the house like she was seeing it for the first time. There was organized, pristine clutter, so many lovely things everywhere, much like the gift shops where she often shopped. Her eyes panned each room, taking a mental inventory, winding up in Cliff's den. The bookcases were lined with business books and publications, biographies, and college trophies; the walls papered with diplomas and accolades. She picked up a photo of Cliff, Brian and Christine with a banner behind them announcing that SterTechCo had attained $1 million in sales. Rita smiled, remembering that day. Cliff had been so proud – of his company, of his kids and yes, of himself. It seemed like a lifetime ago.

And in many ways, it was. Cliff was gone, the kids were no longer at the company, and SterTechCo had slowly started to unravel after the milestone.

What could she do to save SterTechCo, to save herself? Lori's words from the night before came back to her. She was good with people, at creating relationships. Over the years she had met many of the company's clients at technology conferences and recognition banquets and at parties they hosted. She could contact them, talk about the new direction of the company and find out if they'd be interested in their new consulting services. Yes, she could do that. Rita retrieved the portable phone from its cradle on the desk and punched in Christine's cell number.

"Hi, Rita. What's up?"

"Well, Glen, Saleem, Kerry and I had a meeting this morning and decided to concentrate on getting the LA project done. They're obviously our biggest client, and the payoff would be enough to give us some breathing room."

"Sounds like a plan."

"Anyway, Glen is in charge of coordinating that, and I couldn't see any reason to hang around the office, so I came home," Rita said.

"You probably don't know this," Christine said. "But when a deadline was looming and Dad didn't know what to do besides wait and worry, he'd get together with clients, take them to lunch or spring for a round of golf."

"Funny you should mention that. That's exactly what I was thinking of doing – not the golf thing, but meeting with them."

"That's a great idea," Christine said.

"The other day you and Brian mentioned shifting SterTechCo's focus toward consulting," Rita said. "And since I was getting together with them anyway, I thought I'd mention the consulting idea and see if there's any interest."

"Didn't we decide to put that on hold until we got through this crisis?" Christine interrupted.

"Yes, but the more I think about it, the more I believe we're going to make this deliverable, and if we wait, it'll take that much longer to get the consulting practice off the ground. What do you think?" Rita asked.

A few moments ticked by before Christine spoke. "Good point."

"Thanks," Rita said. "So how do you see SterTechCo moving into the consulting business?" There was some commotion on the other end of the phone. "Am I catching you at a bad time?"

"Not really. In the world of technology there's always a crisis," Christine answered, and Rita heard her say to someone, "Tell them I'll be there in a minute." Christine went back to their conversation. "Let's see. Where were we? Oh yes, Brian and I thought SterTechCo should start off with small projects while continuing to market and support the software product."

"How do you find those types of projects?" Rita asked.

"You start with exactly what you're going to do – talk with current clients," Christine said, "Find out if they have some projects coming up. Let them know we'd be interested in bidding on them. Also, for the governmental agencies, you can begin to look for RFPs ... uh ... Request for Proposals for projects that would be doable for our size and resources."

"So about RFPs," Rita began, "where do you look for those?" Several lines rang in the background. "We can talk later, if you'd like."

Christine spoke to someone, but Rita couldn't make out the words. "Yeah, I do have to go, but there are websites which list current RFPs. Check with Kerry."

"I'll do that. Thanks," Rita said.

"You're welcome. Good luck." Christine disconnected.

Rita tapped in Carmen's number. When the other woman answered, Rita asked, "Would you please pull together a list of our clients, contact information, and the projects that we've either completed or are under contract?"

"Will do," she replied.

"Thanks. I'll be in around nine. Would you please connect me with Kerry?"

"Sure. See you in the morning." A couple of beeps and rings later, Rita went over the specifics with Kerry before clicking off. With web addresses written down, Rita fired up the computer. She wasn't exactly sure what she was looking at, but she would print out some possibilities and meet with Kerry tomorrow.

Rita rubbed her eyes and realized the room was dark. Squinting at the digital time in the lower right of the computer screen, she couldn't believe it was eight o'clock. The hours had flown by. She was achy-tired mixed with excitement. For the first time since she blurted out she wanted to be SterTechCo's CEO, Rita was beginning to feel like one, like she had something to contribute; the addition of consulting to SterTech-Co services was just what she needed to make her footprint on the company. And tomorrow she was going to take off running.

Twenty-One

While her numbers fared slightly better for a residential loan than they had on the commercial side, the result was the same. Jade tapped a pencil on the drafting table. So where did that leave her? No bank financing. Even though she suspected the outcome after her own number-crunching, she had hoped some special formula or number manipulation would have yielded a more desirable result. Without traditional financing, the only way she was going to reach her goal of owning income property was seller-financing, and she wasn't sure the Atwoods would be open for that. But even if they agreed to carry the note, what about the down payment? More pencil tapping. She might be able to scrounge up a couple of thousand. Would it be enough? Well, there was only one way to find out. Jade took a deep breath, picked up her cell, scrolled through the list of numbers and hit the call key.

"Hi, Tony. Jade Hastings here."

"Jade. How are you?"

"Good. Say, I was wondering when you might be able to get together to finalize the house deal."

"Well, I'm in town today for a doctor's appointment. Seems like I've been in town more lately than I was all last year."

Jade retrieved her appointment book from her desk and checked the entries. The Bruggeman preliminary plans were due tomorrow morning, and they weren't finished. True to her nature, it was going to be another all-nighter to meet the deadline, so what difference did it make if she took an hour out of the business day to get together with Tony? "I'm flexible. Whatever works for you is fine with me."

"Let's see," Tony said with a pause. "I could meet in a couple of hours at that Starbucks."

"Perfect. See you then." Jade disconnected and attempted to get back to work on the Bruggeman plans, but there was no quashing her preoccupation with the Atwood deal. She did an online search of rents in her area and retrieved her monthly cash flow statement. If the Atwoods would agree to carry the note, and if she could rent her house for close to the mortgage payment … Jade calculated new numbers, recorded the adjustments and examined the bottom line. She'd have to rent her house and fast. But what about the unfinished projects? She tore a fresh yellow sheet of paper from its pad, scribbled a list of tasks and studied it. The house *could* be rentable in a couple of weeks, maybe three, if she called in some favors. That would leave her only about another month before two house payments caused major financial damage. Pretty scary for a single woman who spent a lifetime building a good credit score. She could wait, save some money, pay off some bills, shore up her financials and look for investment property. That sounded pretty good. But the Atwood house would probably be gone. Hmm. Jade checked the time. Just a few more answers to the last few questions, and she'd know soon enough if the deal was going to fly. She grabbed her purse and headed out the door.

~

Jade found Tony seated in the lounging area, sipping a small cup of coffee. "I'm so glad we could get together today. I'm anxious to work this out."

"We are, too," Tony said. "It's not good to have a place sit like that for so long."

"I agree," Jade said, sucking in some air. "First of all, the inspection went well. No surprises."

"Good." Tony nodded.

Jade mirrored his nodding. "That is, as long as it stays residential, which is why I thought I'd move into it."

"You mean, not change it to offices?"

"No, not right now," she said. "A commercial rehab was going to be too expensive for my budget."

Budget. Up until a couple of weeks ago, before the mini money workshops, the word wasn't even in her vocabulary. Now it was part of regular conversation. For years she'd viewed budgets as an older generational concept. Her parents lived on a budget. Mom stayed at home, and Dad worked construction, so they had to pinch pennies and stash cash. If your income was steady and your job secure, what was the point of budgeting? The results of her money homework lately had brought the answer painfully clear, and now a specific case in point was front and center. She was going to have to resort to nonconventional means to obtain the property. "So I've revised my offering price to match your asking price," Jade said.

"That's good news."

Jade took a deep breath and crossed her fingers. "The only caveat to our deal is the financing."

"Oh?"

"Apparently the lender is not comfortable with my financials. So I was wondering if you'd be interested in carrying the mortgage."

"Hmm." He gently swirled his coffee in the bottom of the cup. "I wasn't expecting that. I just assumed you were going to get a loan."

"Me, too," Jade said. "Unfortunately, lending requirements have gotten much stricter because of the sub-prime mortgage business."

"So … are you telling me that the only way you can buy the house is if we carry the loan?"

Jade nodded.

Tony took a sip of coffee and stared off into space. Jade began to sweat. The last few days had been quite sobering for her. She had not been turned down for so much as a credit card since high school, and in matter of days she'd been turned down for a loan not once but twice. Her dad had negotiated a couple of seller-financed mortgages, but Jade didn't think she'd find herself in a position where it was her *only* option. She held her breath.

"When I bought my ranch forty some years ago, my parents thought I was crazy." He chuckled. "I couldn't blame them really. I mean, there was a shack and a whole lot of nothing. But I saw potential. So the old guy who owned it gave me a heck of a deal, and I've managed to build it into something I'm pretty proud of." A smile crossed his face. "Anyhow, someone took a chance on me when I needed it. I suppose it's the least I could do for someone who reminds me of myself in my younger days."

Jade exhaled. "Really? So, you'll carry the mortgage?"

He nodded.

"That's great! But what about your brother and sister? Will they be okay with that?"

His smile broadened. "Don't you worry about them. If nothing else, I'll buy out their part and carry the note myself."

Jade blew a huge sigh of relief.

"There are just a few more details to iron out," Tony said.

"Shoot."

"Well, I don't have to tell you that I'm not young any more." He blushed, almost embarrassed. "And neither are my brother and sister, so carrying a regular thirty-year mortgage won't work for us."

"Okay. We could structure the loan where the total amount would be amortized over a certain number of years like a regular loan with equal payments, but after, say, ten years the note would have to be paid off or renegotiated."

"Let's say, five. At my age, five years is a long time." He winked.

Jade would have preferred ten years. Five was going to be risky. The downturn in the economy and the unprecedented slide in the housing market had everybody a lot more skittish about major financial decisions, including Jade herself. She chewed on her lower lip. The price was good, long-term potential excellent. And how could she ignore the love factor? She loved that house. Seconds ticks by. Then, like a bungee jumper right before falling forward, she squeezed her eyes shut and let go. "Okay. Five years. Anything else?"

"Would you be able to close in 30 days?" Tony asked.

The quick closing date took her aback. "Well, I've got some things I need to take care of." Like getting her house ready to rent, moving and most importantly, figuring out where she was going to get the down payment.

"As you know, settling the estate has taken years, and now my sister is beginning to have second thoughts. She thinks it's some kinda sign that maybe we shouldn't sell it. Anyway, I think the sooner we close, the better."

Where was she going to come up with the down payment in 30 days? If she rented her house quickly, she could use the deposits. What else? Maybe she'd be able to sell enough stuff out of the garage in time. Maybe not. She just didn't have sufficient liquid assets for a down payment. Suddenly the solution hit her. "Remember me telling you that I was doing some work for Mark the attorney I recommended to you?" Tony nodded. "If he is agreeable, and if the numbers jive, would you be open to accepting his fee to settle the estate as the down payment?"

Tony stroked his chin. "Well, well, I suppose if the numbers came out the same, and of course I'd have to run this by my sister and brother."

"I'll check with Mark and get back with you today."

"Okay. I'll wait to hear from you before mentioning it to my family in Phoenix."

Jade rose and hitched her purse on her shoulder. "Thank you. I'm very excited about the house. I'll be in touch this afternoon. Then I think we can finalize the deal." She punctuated the sentence with a firm handshake and a smile.

Tony returned with a quick nod, and she was out the door.

~

The clock on the dashboard reminded Jade there were only a few hours left in the regular work day to get hold of Mark and get a head start on the Bruggeman drawings. She started the engine, dialed the AC to max, flipped open her cell and tapped in Mark's number.

"Jade," Mark answered. "I was just thinking about you."

"All good, I hope."

"Always." The two of them had dated briefly after her divorce. Sex was amazing, but there wasn't a lot of talk afterwards. "Thanks for the referral, by the way. Tony Atwood."

"Actually, he's the reason for my call," Jade said.

"Oh?"

"We've been talking about me buying the house."

"He mentioned that."

"Well, I'm a little short for the down payment," Jade said.

"So you want to know if I can pay you early," Mark interrupted.

"Can you?"

"Unfortunately, I have a couple of clients who owe me some substantial money, so I'm a bit strapped myself."

"Then I may have a solution," Jade said.

"I'm all ears."

"Obviously, I don't know what your fee is for handling the Atwood estate, but if it's close to my fee for your new office plans, we could trade. My services pay you on behalf of the Atwoods, which will be the down payment on the house. You won't have to come up with cash to pay me, the estate gets settled, and the Atwoods come out financially the same."

Jade could imagine Mark's brain churning. "Okay. I get it. Yeah, that works for me. What did Tony say?"

"I told him I'd run it by you first, and if you were on board, he'd speak with his siblings."

"Let me know."

"Will do." Jade disconnected and immediately called Tony to give him an update. He'd get back with her, but he was fairly confident they would go for it.

This was really happening, she thought. A swirl of emotions went into motion – excitement, fear, panic. There was still time to pull the plug on this transaction. Why this house? Why now? Why stir up the status quo of her comfortable, non-chaotic life? Because it was time – time to take control of her finances and her life. Her eyes glanced over to the clock again, and it was time to get back to work.

Go to the Appendix for the article entitled **Alternative Financing for Real Estate**.

Twenty-Two

"No, Bob, we don't *need* an umbrella." Lori's voice was strained. "And certainly *not* a $400 one."

Bob had gone to Home Depot for light bulbs and a garden hose. Lori mentally kicked herself for asking him to go – he wasn't capable of sticking to a shopping list.

"It's on sale, and it'll go great in the back yard," he bargained.

"I don't care if it's on sale. Remember our deal?" At least he'd called, she thought. Two weeks ago he would have had it set up before she got home.

"Oh, yeah."

Just over a week into their financial agreement, and things were not going well. A check of recent credit card charges revealed that Bob had purchased something online and withdrawn cash from their checking account on top of their agreed upon weekly allowance. Lori was frustrated, angry and tired of the repetitive conversations about money, but yet they were headed for another one.

"Are you on your way home?" she asked.

"Pretty much," he answered. "I just have to stop for gas."

"I've just got to pick up the girls, so we'll probably get home about the same time. See you then." She clicked off.

What was she going to do? Making a game of it wasn't working. Appealing to his sense of obligation was like talking to a wall. Maybe she should try the total financial control angle – take away his ATM card and all of his credit cards and dole out the weekly allowance. Of course with their stellar credit, he always could get other cards. She shook her head. The bottom line was that there was no controlling him or his behavior. The only option left was to explain how she was feeling and up the ante.

The girls were waiting outside of their school when Lori pulled up. They climbed into the late model SUV and began jabbering about their day. Lori smiled. Fridays were her favorite day of the week. It was Bob's night off and the only one void of practices and recitals. They ate fried chicken and garlic toast at Lucky Wishbone, like she had done with her parents, and then usually watched a DVD. After the craziness of the week, Fridays were a welcomed respite. Somewhere along the line their lives had become one giant calendar-driven blur complete with and individu- ally color-coded activity and chore lists. Orchestrated chaos is what she called it, and it was coming with an expensive price tag. Between the girls' after-school and weekend activities and their work schedules, there was little family time and more dollars spent on the latest "need" for soccer, piano lessons, karate, and dance – and of course Bob's weekly "gotta have." The girls seemed to like their activities, but were they overcommitted? How much was too much? Wasn't down time important, too?

Shortly after Lori had ushered the girls into the house to play in their rooms, Bob walked through the back door with a Home Depot shopping bag straining from the weight of its contents.

Lori closed her eyes. "What's in the bag?"

"The stuff we needed from Home Depot," he responded and set the bag on the counter with a clunk.

"We talked about light bulbs and a hose. It doesn't look or sound like either one of those." Lori stared at the bag.

He planted both feet firmly on the ground and faced her. His tone was strained. "I put the hose in the garage, and I needed a couple of things to finish some projects around the house. I thought that'd make you happy."

"The deal was *nothing* except for gas and food unless we talked about it," she said.

"This is crazy. I should be able to go to the store and buy a few things without getting the third degree." His voice reached an angry whisper.

"A deal is a deal. If we needed something else from Home Depot, we should have discussed it."

"A couple of dollars isn't going to break us," he retorted.

Right on cue – there was the rationale, she thought. "You're right. One purchase by itself isn't a big deal, but it's not just one purchase. Remember looking at the credit card bill and making the comment that you didn't think you charged that much?" He frowned and remained tight-lipped. "That's how that happens. A few dollars here and there, and before you know it, it's hundreds of dollars." She stopped long enough for more justifications from him, but none came. "Speaking of credit cards, I checked online today, and there's a new charge from some company back east. What's that about?"

"Now you're spying on me?" His jaw tightened, and his eyes widened.

"I discovered you'd made an ATM withdrawal today, so yes, I checked the credit card activity." The confrontation was met with a long silence. "We're supposed to be *selling*, not buying," Lori said. "And do you want to explain the cash withdrawal? What happened to the deal we had about a weekly allowance?"

The motor on the refrigerator hummed, and the ice maker dumped while the seconds ticked and Lori waited. It appeared her suspicions about her husband's quick agreement last week were correct. He had stroked her with pure tripe to put an end to the conversation. Nothing had changed.

"Well, I was flipping through the channels the other day and came across this yard maintenance tool set. It was such a great deal," Bob said. Lori gave him the *I-can't-believe-what-I'm-hearing* look. "Come on, it was only a couple of payments, and it'll be perfect to take care of the yard." Her expression remained steadfast. "And I had to pay back the money I borrowed from Faye a couple of weeks ago."

"Apparently, I was the only one on board with the deal we made last week." Her lips were pressed so tightly together the words barely escaped.

"It all made sense when we talked about it, but now doing it doesn't feel right," Bob said. "I mean, a grown man on an allowance and being told what he can and cannot buy without discussing it with his wife?"

"So you think this is about you?"

"Isn't it?"

"No, this is about our family," Lori said. The comment brought a frown to Bob's face. "We can't continue to spend our money in a vacuum without consideration for other factors."

"What do you mean?"

"If something happened to either one of us, we would not be able to support our family." Lori paused and let the picture settle for a moment. "This nonsensical spending must stop. We must stick to our plan."

Bob leaned against the counter, crossed his arms and tucked his chin closer to his chest. "I don't know why you've gotten so gung ho on us doing this financial planning. When we first got married, we used to have so much fun. You didn't seem to have a problem spending money. Now suddenly, I'm the bad guy because I haven't jumped on this financial bandwagon of yours."

"We were young. Back then we could afford to make some mistakes with our money," Lori began. "It's different now. We've got two girls and a mortgage, and I'd like to retire someday, which is going to be here before we know it. The bottom line is we've been working our tails off for all these years together, and we're basically in the same financial position we were when we first got married. Doesn't that bother you?"

"I told you before – that is your area of expertise, not mine," Bob said. "I see we've got a house, two cars, and we go on vacation every year, and I'm happy with that. Why can't you be?"

"We owe about what the house and cars are worth. And the vacation is paid with credit cards until we work a lot of extra hours for months to pay it off." Lori took a breath. "I can't be happy continuing to live day-by-day, waiting for a financial disaster to hit that could wipe us out."

"There you go being melodramatic again." He rolled his eyes.

"No, I'm not," Lori retorted. "Weren't you just telling me about that guy at work who got hurt on the job and had to medically retire?"

"Well, yeah," he said with a shrug. "But he's going to get disability."

"At a fraction of his current salary."

"He'll probably be okay."

"I don't know if he's going to be okay financially," Lori said. "But I *do* know if we lost part of your salary, we'd be in bad shape."

"You're smart. You'd figure it out." Bob opened the refrigerator door. "I'm hungry. When are we going to Lucky Wishbone?"

Lori blew out a sigh and stared at her husband. The differences in their attitudes toward money were deepening. A sickening feeling formed in the pit of her stomach as the reality of their personal financial disparity began to sink in. Would there ever be a financial meeting of the minds? Was Bob capable of being fiscally responsible? How long could she, should she, continue in this financial tug-of-war? "In a minute. We've got to get back on track here."

Bob shut the door and faced her. His tone was sharp. "What do you want from me?"

"I want us to stick to our deal." The two squared off like gunfighters on a dusty western street.

"Or?" Bob asked.

"If you're not willing to work together on this, then I'm not sure where that leaves us as a couple."

The statement might as well have been a bullet to the chest. His eyes widened, and his chin inched forward. "What? Over a couple of dollars?"

"No, over trust," Lori answered. "You broke your promise, not once but twice in a week. If we don't have trust, respect and communication, then what's left to keep this marriage going?"

Seconds ticked by while he processed the concept and the question. "I hadn't thought of it that way." He drew her close to him and hugged her hard. "I'm sorry. I don't want anything to happen to us."

"Me, either." She closed her eyes and hugged him back. She wanted this to work more than anything – the marriage, their financial plan.

There were so many things she loved about him. He was a hard worker and a great father. Unfortunately, if his financial improprieties continued .... She shook off the rest of the thought. For now she wanted to believe he finally realized how serious their situation was. For the sake of her family she had to give him another chance. "So we're back on track?"

"Yes. Promise."

She looked into his eyes hard and straight. "I hope so." Lori gave her husband a squeeze. "Let's get something to eat."

Twenty-Three

Jade was brain-dead, butt-dragging tired. Between pulling an all-nighter to get the Bruggeman plans finished and pinching herself for an hour through the presentation to keep awake, she was ready to call it a day. She squinted at the wall clock. Only ten-thirty. She was contemplating her options for the rest of the day when her cell phone rang.

"You've got a deal."

The news drove her heart into her throat, rendering her speechless.

"Are you there?" Tony asked Jade.

"Yes, yes! You just caught me by surprise, that's all."

"Good. So I guess the next step is to prepare a contract, right?" Tony questioned. Yikes! A contract. This was real. This was really happening.

"When do you think you could do that?"

"Uh." Jade thought. "Let me give Mark a call, and I'll call you right back." She disconnected and immediately got hold of Mark. Yes, he could have it ready that afternoon. The arrangements to meet at Mark's office worked for everybody, so it was set.

The good news about the Atwood house was like a shot of adrenaline, and the tick of the thirty-day-closing clock reminded her she had no time to lose.

Jade tapped on her boss's door and asked Barbara, "Got a minute?"

"Come on in." Barbara removed her readers and laid them on the stack of papers in front of her. Jade took a seat. The two had become friends over the years since Barbara hired her fresh out of the college.

"New glasses?" Jade asked.

"Yes. Wait 'til you get to my age. I had 20-20 vision until I went pre-menopausal."

"Yeah, I'm looking forward to that, all right," Jade said with an eye roll.

"By the way, good job on the Bruggeman project. He's very happy. It probably means a lot more business coming our way." Barbara slid back in her seat and interlaced her fingers on her lap. "So what's up?"

"I was hoping I could take a week or so off."

Barbara leaned forward, and there was concern in her tone. "Is everything okay?" The only time Jade took off was toward the end of the year when leave days were going to expire, and even then she usually left a few on the books.

"Oh, yes." Jade said with a flick of her wrist. "I bought a house around the corner from here, so I've got to get my place ready to rent."

"What? I didn't know you were looking for a new place."

A smile came over Jade's face. "I wasn't. You know how they say that a pet picks you? Well, this house picked me. I found it on the way to work not too long ago, and everything fell into place. The sellers want a short closing date, so I've got a lot of work to do between now and then."

"That's fast. Are you sure? I mean, that's such a big decision," Barbara said.

"Saying it out loud does make it sound rather impulsive," Jade said, "but I've done my homework. The numbers work all the way around, and with house prices where they are, I think it's a good time to buy."

Barbara's eyes grew wide, and she shook her head. "I have to say, you've got more guts than I do. It sounds risky to me."

"I'm sure you got some raised eyebrows when you decided to start this business," Jade said. "Walking out on a steady paycheck with a growing firm might have been viewed as a little risky."

A smile crossed Barbara's face. "Okay. I get it – different kinds of risks, different comfort levels."

"Exactly," Jade said.

"I'll keep my fingers crossed for you." Barbara grabbed a sheet of paper from the credenza behind her. "Looks like I can spare you for a week, but that's all. We've got some large projects coming up."

"I'll make it work." Jade rose from her chair. "Thanks."

"No problem. See you in a week."

Jade snatched her purse and the briefcase nestled alongside the file cabinet in her office and headed for her car. She punched in Brian's number. "Hi, Brian. It's Jade."

"Hey, Jade. What's up?"

"Well, I know this is short notice, but what are doing after work today?"

"Nothing. What do you have in mind?"

She took a breath. "I could use your help in organizing my rehab projects so I can get them finished in the next 30 days."

"What's the rush?" Brian asked.

Jade pulled into traffic. "I bought another house, and I've got to get mine ready to rent."

"Really? You're moving? Where?" His surprise sizzled through the phone.

She should get used to that reaction. Friends and family were going to be plenty shocked when she announced her plans. And who could blame them? Jade had been in her present home for only five years, which was short-term for those closest to her. Most of them were still living in their first house, and she didn't know anybody who had a rental. Yes, she was definitely bucking tradition. And yes, there was going to be a lot of explaining to do. "Yep, downtown. I'll give you all the details when I see you."

"Okay," Brian said. "I can probably be there about 5:30."

"Sounds great. Thanks." Jade clicked off and glanced at her speedometer. She let up on the accelerator and panned the area for cops and speed enforcement cameras. There had been more traffic stops in her life than she cared to count – par for the course when you're perpetually late. She reprimanded herself for not paying more attention. There was neither the time for traffic school nor the money for another ticket. Jade pulled into her driveway and opened the garage door with her remote. For a moment Jade sat in her car and stared at the enormity of the task before her. Not only did she have projects to complete, she had to purge and pack the accumulation of three generations' worth of stuff. Ever since her parents' house reached capacity, her garage had become the resting place for her family's treasures … and junk. She sighed and lifted herself out of the car. Well, it wasn't going to sort itself.

Jade snaked through the garage and made a peanut butter sandwich on the way to her bedroom and a quick change of clothes. Back in the garage Jade stuffed the last bite into her mouth as she snatched a clipboard from the workbench and made columns – *craigslist*, Atwood house, current projects, and give-away – and designated areas in the garage for each category. Jade lifted, examined, evaluated and shoved boxes and materials, most of which she had forgotten she had, inherited leftovers from her dad's projects. Some were going to work quite nicely in the new house. The lure of more usable surprises kept her plugging along until she happened to glance at her watch. "Omigod! Look what time it is! I've got to get going."

Jade jumped into her car. "This is good. This is right." The mantra began to play in her head during a series of green lights, but was quickly interrupted by troubling questions. What if she couldn't get her house rented soon? What if she came across major issues with the Atwood house? What if some unforeseen event rocked the status quo of the rest of her financial life? Worry and doubt slowed her drive to a crawl until she found herself stopped in front of Mark's office. A few more gloom and doom "what-ifs" made their way around her psyche before Jade gave them a good shake. That was enough of that, she thought. *If* anything came up, she'd deal with it. This was an opportunity she wasn't going to pass up for all the never ending "what-ifs."

"They're waiting for you in the conference room," Mark's receptionist greeted Jade.

"Thanks, Kim," she said as she passed.

All the men rose when Jade walked in. "Sorry I'm late."

"Actually you're right on time," Mark said.

"So I am," Jade said, much to her surprise and judging from the look on Mark's face, his as well.

Tony Atwood stepped aside to reveal another man beside him. "Jade, this is my brother, Frank. Frank, Jade." They shook hands and *how-do-you-dos* went around the table. Then the brothers introduced their sister, Amelia, who stayed seated at the table. Her handshake surprised Jade. For such a petite woman her grip was firm and purposeful. They exchanged pleasantries and everyone sat down.

Mark handed a document to Jade. "The Atwoods have reviewed the offer, and it represents what they believe has been verbally agreed upon. Why don't you read it over and tell us if it's acceptable."

Jade read and mentally checked off the terms. Tony was going to carry the note. Good interest rate. Yes, this was it. Everything looked in order. "Looks good to me."

She picked up the pen, took a deep breath, signed and passed it to Frank on her right. After Tony and Amelia signed, Mark left the room and returned shortly with copies for everyone.

"I guess we'll meet back up in 30 days to finalize everything, right?" Frank asked.

"Right," Mark answered. "The title agency will do a title search, set up the account to handle the payments, and make sure everything's in order for closing."

Jade rose. "Sorry to sign and go, but I've got a lot of work to do." She made eye contact with each of the Atwoods. "Thank you so much for trusting me with this house. I know it meant a lot to all of you. I won't let you down."

Extending his hand, Tony spoke for the group. "We believe you'll take good care of it."

"I will," she said, shaking his hand and nodding to Frank and Amelia. "See you in a month."

~

When Brian arrived, he found the garage door open and Jade knee-deep in boxes. He was dressed in casual Friday attire – pressed tailored jeans and yellow golf shirt. Whatever mousse had held his hair together in the morning had succumbed to the day's elements and drooped along one cheekbone. "Wow. It didn't look like there was quite this much stuff in here when I helped you move the vanity the other day."

She stopped, placed hands on hips and surveyed the work in process. "Probably because I had everything stacked nice and neat. Believe it or not, there is a method to this madness."

"Need any help?" he asked across the cardboard chaos.

"I'm afraid this is pretty much up to me," she answered. "But let's go in the house and take a look at what I *could* use your help with."

Brian picked a path of least resistance and met Jade at the back door. The pair maneuvered around piles of construction materials which had been in limbo so long that a thick film of dust masked their condition.

"Can I get you something to drink?" Jade pulled open the door on the refrigerator and stuck her head inside. "I've got water, ice tea, beer, wine."

"Beer is good," Brian said, taking a seat at the kitchen table.

Jade retrieved a bottle for each of them, twisted the caps, handed one bottle to Brian and sat down at the table with the other. "Thanks again for coming on such short notice. I really appreciate it."

"No problem. What's going on?"

She took a sip of beer, then set it on the table. "The short of the long of it is that I came across this old house downtown that I eventually want to turn into professional space, but in the meantime I'm going to live in it. There are some special provisions for a conversion to commercial if it's been your residence for two years. Anyway, one of the reasons I wanted to buy that house was for rental income. Since I can't convert that one for a while, I thought I'd switch this one to a rental. The owners want to close in 30 days, and I'm feeling a little overwhelmed. I could sure use your help in developing a completion schedule for this place."

Brian nodded and took a long pull on his beer. "Sure. I can do that. I didn't know you were interested in becoming a landlord."

"Finding that house downtown really got me thinking." Jade stared at the bubbles in the amber bottle. "Dad worked hard all his life, and in the end he didn't have a lot to show for it. If he had turned even a few of those houses he rehabbed into rentals, he wouldn't have had to worry so much about how he was going to pay the bills when construction work slowed around here. Mom would be better off financially now, too."

"Why do you think he *didn't* go the rental route?" Brian asked.

"He considered rentals investment property," Jade explained. "Rich people invested; he fixed up houses and got paid when he sold them, like a second job."

"But you're not in the same situation as your dad. You have a stable job that pays well. Why go through the hassle of being a landlord when you don't need the income?" he asked.

Jade thought back to what Lori had said at one of their lunch meetings: many times appearances couldn't be further from the truth. In Jade's case that truth had her scared. Work had been sporadic lately, and a couple of times she wasn't sure whether Barbara was going to be forced to lay her off. Without a job, her obligations would bury her in a matter of months. It was about time she put her knowledge of real estate to work toward building a sound financial future that wasn't predicated strictly on steady employment.

"Right now work is going okay, but nothing's for sure," Jade answered. "I know real estate, and I think it's a good investment. It appreciates in value over time, and it can generate income. Honestly, I don't know why I've waited so long to get started in the rental business."

"Isn't it a hassle though?" Brian asked. "Getting good tenants who'll pay on time and not mess up the place? Then there's keeping up with the repairs. If someone is paying you, you've got to respond quickly."

"You're right – good tenants are the key." Jade mulled this idea over. How did one find the right one? Check their credit, employment, references? She hadn't really thought about the logistics of being a landlord. She made a mental note to do some research. "No doubt owning rental property can have its challenges, but I believe the long-term benefits will outweigh the short-term hassles."

Brian began slowly, as though his thoughts were still forming. "Maybe it's time I buy a house. I'm getting some money from Dad's estate that would make a nice down payment."

"That's a great idea!" Jade said. "There are some really good deals right now."

"It's too bad you're stuck on turning this one into a rental," Brian said. "I love the area, and I think it'd be perfect for me."

She *did* have her mind set on renting it, but the proposal sent Jade's mind into motion – sell versus lease. One less mortgage, no tenant hassle, and Brian would probably finish the projects. Left brain told her that the proposition made sense. Right brain screamed to wait a minute! Did she really want to sell? What happened to her goal of having income property? If not now, then when? Umh. "I agree – it's a great house in a great neighborhood, but I really want to rent it."

Brian shrugged. "Well, if you change your mind … ."

"I'll let you know." Jade took a breath. "Ready to get started?"

"Sure am."

"Let me see – where did I put my list?" She drummed her finger-nails on the table. "I'll be right back." Jade sprinted to the garage where she snatched the clipboard. Then she retrieved the project list from her purse, sat down, and handed the list to Brian.

He stared down at the list. "The kitchen is obviously the biggest project. The cabinets need to be painted. The back splash, countertop and sink need to be installed. The shower needs to be tiled, and both the shower and floor need to be grouted. I would paint the inside and power-wash the outside. You have here to replace the carpet, but I'd clean it and see what it looks like. No sense replacing the windows and exterior doors at this point, but caulking all the way around would be a good idea. They're in good shape. Yeah, if we work together, I think we can knock these out pretty quick."

"I was planning on doing this solo," Jade said.

Brian shook his head. "There's no way you're going to get all this done by yourself in 30 days. Really. I'm glad to help you out."

Jade sucked in some air. She wasn't used to asking for help. "Independent" may not have been her given middle name, but it might as well have been. "I couldn't ask you to do that. I don't have money to pay you, and it just wouldn't seem right."

Brian looked up, and his expression softened. "Don't worry about any of that right now. We'll figure something out."

She couldn't believe what she was hearing. Rita had always said he was a nice guy, but this kind of generosity toward someone he hardly knew was simply overwhelming. She paused. Was he being helpful, or was he hitting on her? Had she been out of the dating scene so long she had forgotten what flirting looked like? She squinted into his eyes for any hints. Boy, she *was* clueless. "Brian, I don't know what to say." He looked away, and she didn't as he took another long pull on his beer. His cheeks began to turn a soft crimson. What was that about? What if he *was* attracted to her? Would that be so bad? Gorgeous and sweet with a bit of innocence thrown in. And young. There was an age difference. Stay focused, she reminded herself. There was a lot of work to do in a short amount of time.

"Aw, it's nothing. Of course I'm back to work at the accounting firm, so I only have after five and weekends."

"I'm grateful for whatever help you can give me," Jade said. "I've taken a week off, so let's see how we can divide these projects into those I can do myself and those we'll do together."

"Sounds like a plan." With that Jade moved close to him, grabbed the clipboard and pen, and began to study the piece of paper he was still holding. His gaze shifted from her to the list. "Let's mark a 'one' or 'two' next to each item for the number of people per project, and then we can prioritize each group. Also, we'll make sure you have everything you need to complete the project and make a list of necessary materials."

Jade nodded in agreement, and they went to work.

Two hours, two Lucky's combo plates, and a couple beers later, she was feeling fairly optimistic that she was going to have a rentable house in 30 days. Of course rentable didn't mean rented.

She said goodnight to Brian, with his promise of returning bright and early the next day, and padded off to bed. Most of the projects would be done in the next couple of weeks, so she could begin to advertise. Who was her target market? Was there a specific area or place she could focus to increase the chances of a quick lease? She allowed the questions to settle inside her head as she crawled between the sheets and drifted off the sleep.

---

*Go to the Appendix for the article entitled **Good Tenants – How to Find Them and How to Keep Them**.*

Twenty-Four

As Lori prepared the conference room for the lunch meeting with the girls, she reflected on the weekend's activities around the house. Angela and Taunya had cleaned their rooms of four large bags of toys, dolls, clothes and stuffed animals for the local abuse shelter, which they accomplished virtually unsupervised. She was so proud of them. They far exceeded her expectations both in number and in their choices. Many items were practically new, yet the girls wanted to give them away. If only the rest of the purging had gone as smoothly. Bob challenged almost every item. The length of the challenge was determined by the degree of attachment, and it became apparent early on Bob was attached to a lot. The process droned on. Lori stayed on task and pushed her husband onward. By late Sunday afternoon the section of the garage containing items designated for sale was respectable for the first pass-through. The small victory had not come without a price though. The verbal tug-of-war over each item left her exhausted to start the work week.

Lori positioned pads of paper and pencils in front of four chairs and stationed glasses and a pitcher of water in the center of the table. As much as she wanted to believe Bob, she wasn't sure he was capable of changing. Money attitudes ran deep, born out of a family's financial history and values and peer pressure. In Bob's case she was bucking forty years of watching his father scrape by – spending money when he had it, borrowing from friends and family when he didn't and dying with more debt than possessions – and a lifetime of trying to keep up with his friends who shared the same money mentality.

"Hello," the voice echoed through the office.

"In here, Marla," Lori yelled.

Marla appeared in the conference room, deposited her lunch and purse on the table and gave Lori a hug. "Why don't you come with me into the kitchen and tell me how things are going?" Lori said to Marla.

"For such a simple idea I didn't know how involved everything was going to get," Marla started. The two women reached the break room, and Lori busied herself heating up a container of leftovers in the microwave.

"Yoo-hoo. Where is everybody?"

"In the kitchen, Jade," Lori shouted.

Jade's appearance took her friends by surprise. Her T-shirt and jeans were covered in different colors of paint, and tiny specks of the morning's project dotted her face and hair.

"I take it you're not working at the office today," Lori said.

"No. I made an offer on that house I told you guys about, and they accepted," she answered while popping the lid off of her plastic container.

"Hello." Rita's voice carried through the quiet office.

"Kitchen," the group answered in unison.

Hugs made the rounds, except for Jade who could only reasonably assure them that most of the paint she was wearing was dry. The last of the lunches was removed from the microwave, and everyone began to make their way down the hall toward the conference room.

"So, Marla, you started to tell me about how things were going with the new business," Lori said as the friends settled into their chairs.

"Like I was saying, I wouldn't have imagined that such a simple idea would be so much work to bring it to market."

Jade scraped some dried paint from her forearms. "From our last discussion it sounded like you had your supplies pretty much lined up and just needed to figure out how you were going to reproduce the sketches."

"More or less," Marla answered. "The search on the Internet for the lowest prices on paint and brushes took a lot longer than I anticipated – partially because I hadn't done much research on the Web and partially because there are so many websites offering an extensive number of art supplies. Turns out no one company has everything I need at the lowest price for each item, so I'm going to have to use several companies." She paused long enough to take a bite of her salad. "Then there was the decision of what type of material I was going to use. That process took hours. At first I thought I'd have the sketch reproduced on canvas. I took a sample of canvas paper around to the various printers, only to learn they use rolls of canvas which is cut to specifications. Too expensive. Then I decided to use paper which would be heavy enough to support acrylic paint yet light enough to be used in a copier. After several stops I finally found a printer who could copy the sketch, but only if the paper was less than 110-pound. Doable." Marla stopped again. "Am I talking too much? Am I boring you guys?"

"No, no," Rita said. "I'm interested in hearing the story."

"Me, too," Jade piped in. "Good problem solving. Are you ready to go then?"

Marla poured herself a glass of water. "Almost. I've got to take pictures of the sketches, paint some as examples and then take pictures of them to post on *eBay*."

"When do you think you'll be able to go live?" Rita asked.

"Maybe a week or two. My friend, Rachel, said she'd help. Come to find out, she's always wanted to learn how to paint, and she loves my idea."

"That's great." Lori poised her fork over the plate of chicken enchiladas. "Is her mom going to set up the accounting?"

Marla nodded in excitement. "She's coming over this week."

"Perfect. Better sooner than later," Lori said. "And, Jade, you said you're buying that house you told us about?"

The question caught her chewing her last bite of lunch, which she quickly swallowed. "Yes. I took off this week so I can finish the projects around my house to get it ready to rent and to pack."

"I thought you were going to rent the new place," Rita said. "Go the commercial route."

"That was the plan, but … ," Jade stopped. It was one thing to be part of a communal confession about the state of her financial net worth and quite another to admit the bank turned her down not once but twice. When an institution tells you you're in bad shape, you've graduated from speculation to confirmation.

"But?" Rita leaned forward.

"I didn't qualify."

"How are you buying the house then?" Marla asked.

"The seller is carrying the note."

Marla fidgeted in her seat. "That's sounds really risky to me."

Jade agreed. "There's some risk involved, but I've been doing a lot of thinking lately, and it's time I do something to turn my finances and my life around – starting with the Atwood house. I need to get some rent money coming in from my house and the apartment above the carriage house in case something happens to me or my job. And even though I like working for Barbara, I'd like to be able to branch out on my own." There. She'd said it out loud. And it felt right. She wasn't sure of the details yet, but she was sure they would work out if she stayed focused on the plan.

"Sounds like you've done a lot more than just thinking," Lori said. "You've got some goals you're putting into motion. If we can do anything, let us know." She nodded to Rita and Marla, and they agreed.

"Brian volunteered to help me out with the unfinished projects, so I think I'll make the thirty-day deadline for the move to the new house and hopefully have tenants lined up to move in behind me." She paused. "Speaking of tenants, you wouldn't happen to know anybody who's looking for a place to rent, would you?"

"Not off the top of my head," Rita said after giving the question some thought. "But I could put up a notice on the break room bulletin board."

"And I could ask around school," Marla added.

"Great ideas," Lori said. "Where else could you advertise? Think about the location of the house. Are there people who work in the area who might want to rent your house?"

"Of course the first place that pops into my head is the medical center."

"Good one," Lori said. "There are students and the regular staff, and I think they may even employ traveling medical personnel, who work for a year at a time."

"Hmm. That sounds good. I'll contact human resources today. Thanks. And I'll put a flyer together."

Rita piped in. "Can't you advertise that on *craigslist*?"

"Yes, you can," Lori said. "Good idea."

"Thanks, everybody," Jade chimed in, then allowed herself to relax a bit for the first time since she laid eyes on the Atwood house. Between Brian's help and her friends' tenant suggestions, she was beginning to believe she was going to pull off this rental plan.

"Rita, you've been pretty quiet today," Lori started. "What's been going on with you?"

"I finally got the insurance check Saturday," she answered with a lackluster tone.

"That's great," Lori said. "You've been waiting a long time for that. I thought you'd be happier."

"Oh, don't get me wrong. I'm glad to have it, but unfortunately, there are more people with their hands out than there is money to go around." Rita pushed her meal away and dabbed her mouth with her napkin.

"What's going on at SterTechCo?" Jade asked.

Rita took a deep breath. "I check in with Glen twice a day for a status report. Without any major snafus, the majority of the LA project will be done in three weeks. The problem is that payment is net 30, which means it's going to take a month to get paid, and that leaves us a week short to meet payroll and the other monthly obligations." She paused. "I'm beginning to understand why Cliff ended up putting so much of our personal money into the business. I'm afraid I'm going to have to do the same thing."

"So you're thinking you'll pay SterTechCo expenses out of the insurance money?" Lori asked with a hard swallow.

"I don't want to. I've got enough personal bills to go through that sum in no time. But I may not have a choice if I want to keep the company going." Since Saturday, Rita had done nothing but think about how she was going to divide the insurance check. The first round of calculations made it painfully clear that there wasn't enough to meet all of the pressing obligations at SterTechCo and her personal debt. So the rest of the weekend was spent trying to figure out what she was going to do about it. Perhaps a couple of bills could be postponed. There was Cliff's IRA money, which Lori said was an absolute last resort. Was she there yet? The kids probably got their insurance checks, too. Did she want to ask them for help? No. They weren't keen on the whole saving the company idea in the first place. There had to be another way

"Have you talked to Glen and the office manager ... what's her name? Michelle?" Lori asked.

Rita shook her head. "Not yet, but I will as soon as I get back to the office. Glen was occupied with the technical disaster du jour this morning."

"After you've met with them, let me know if there's anything I can do," Lori said. "My concern is that there may come a time when it may not make sense to keep pumping money into a sinking ship."

"Oh, mine, too," Rita responded. "The thought has been eating away at me as we approach this deadline, wondering if we're already there. It was going to be part of my discussion with Glen." Brian and Christine had warned her. SterTechCo problems ran deep. Pouring over the numbers the last two days made her question whether any infusion of money was going to be too little, too late.

"Good. Keep me posted." Lori checked the time. "It sounds like everybody's got quite a bit on their plates. How about we leave our next lunch meeting date open?"

Marla raised her hand. "Wait a minute. Before we wrap it up, everyone's been on the hot seat today but you. How's it going with Bob?"

Lori hoped no one had noticed. She wasn't sure how she felt about Bob, let alone how to explain it to anybody else. These were her friends, but she was still trying to sort everything out. She let as much time tick by as she could without making the situation seem uncomfortable. "We made some progress over the weekend around the house." Lori struggled to come up with other positive things to say.

"And?" Rita asked.

"There's a pile of stuff for him to sell."

"What's going on?" Rita persisted. "What aren't you telling us?"

They had been friends too long. Evasiveness didn't cut it. "He just doesn't want to work together on our finances," Lori began, shaking her head. "He doesn't see the connection between his spending and our financial future and thinks I'm being over-dramatic. In his world our financial situation is just fine the way it is, and I feel like I'm getting sucked into some financial black hole."

"Sounds serious. What are you going to do?" Jade asked.

"Good question. I don't know."

The room fell silent.

"You're not thinking about leaving Bob, are you?" Marla finally asked.

"It has crossed my mind," Lori answered, then quickly added, "but it's complicated. There are so many things to consider."

"I'm sure the girls are a big part of your decision," Marla jumped in. "I know it would be for me."

Lori nodded. "I am concerned how a divorce would affect them. When my parents separated, I was already in high school with a part-time job, so I don't think it affected me as much as maybe it would have if I'd been a lot younger. Bob and the girls are very close. It would be so hard for them to be apart." That was the gut-wrenching part. He may not have been very good at saving money, but he couldn't have been better at spending quality time with Angela and Taunya. He helped with homework, went to all their events and played games with them – so much so that at times Lori thought she really had three children. If only he would be fiscally responsible. "Of course there's the financial end of it," Lori continued after the mental sidebar.

A frown came over Marla. "If the main problem between you two is your differences about money, then why wouldn't a divorce take care of that? Your finances would be separate, right?"

"Yes, but what I meant was that divorce is very expensive." Marla's quizzical expression remained unchanged, so Lori continued. "It's expensive because when you split income and assets, everybody loses financially. There are two households to maintain, which obviously costs more than one, and even under the most amicable circumstances when assets are divided, the piles are rarely equal. It's almost like you're starting from scratch."

"I hadn't really thought of it that way before," Marla said.

"There's a lot to consider, which is why I'm working with Bob as much as I can. We'll have to wait and see what happens." Lori paused for a moment before changing gears. "As I was saying, it sounds like we have a lot of work to do in the next few weeks, so let's leave our next meeting date open, but how about we check in with each other periodically?" Nods went around the room. "Good." Lori took a deep breath. "Don't look so glum, everybody."

"It's sad, that's all, you and Bob having problems," Marla said.

"I know," Lori agreed. When she wasn't upset at her husband's behavior, she was sad, too. They had been together a long time. "But his spending has been a sore spot for us for a long time, and it's getting worse. I just can't take it anymore."

"Sorry to hear that," Rita said.

"Me, too," Jade added. "You've sort of joked about how he spent money. I had no idea it was so serious."

Lori refilled her water glass. "I kept thinking maybe one day he would just wake up financially mature. That day hasn't come, and at this point I don't think it ever will. He buys things as though he were still single without consideration whatsoever for how his behavior affects the rest of the family." She took a breath. "I want more out of life than working my ass off to get to the next month, then start the madness all over again."

"What would you like to do?" Rita asked.

Lori made eye contact with each of her friends, leaned forward to close the gap between them, and whispered, "I've been writing."

"Really? Like the great American novel?" Marla asked.

She blushed. "Oh, I doubt that. It's just a story that popped into my head a few years ago."

"Do tell," Jade urged.

Lori shook her head. "Right now it's not much. I promise as soon as I know it's going somewhere, you three will be the first to know."

"That's exciting." Rita smiled. "I didn't know you wanted to write."

"I like words, and I've read a lot, so I thought *what the hell*," Lori said. "It may not go anywhere, but I'm enjoying the process. I get up at four in the morning and tap away on the computer until the girls wake up. I also grab whatever time I can throughout the day to get a couple of paragraphs down."

"Very cool," Jade said.

Lori checked the time. "Speaking of which, it looks like I've got a couple of minutes before my next client, so if you'll excuse me, I think I'll write a while. Are we agreed to touch base with one another?" Everyone nodded. "And maybe we'll schedule a meeting after our deadlines have been met?" Another collective nod followed. "Then, ladies, we're adjourned. Good luck."

Twenty-Five

Rita was in the middle of her daily afternoon pacing sequence when Glen strode into her office.

"How's it going?" she asked him, not caring to hide the worry on her face.

He collapsed in the leather arm chair angled in front of her desk. The long hours he'd been keeping were etched in the bags under his eyes. "Everybody's working night and day. It's all we can do. Honestly, it's going to be close."

She took the chair opposite him. "We've got to have a Plan B. What if we don't make the LA project deadline? Or what if we meet the deadline, but the check doesn't get here in time to make payroll?"

They stared at each other, both realizing perhaps they were exactly where they'd hoped they wouldn't be. "I know. I haven't been able to think about anything but that. Any ideas?" he asked, arching an eyebrow.

"Let's get together with Michelle and figure out what's absolutely critical. Maybe there are a few bills that can be postponed until the LA check comes in. Hopefully, we'll only be a few weeks short at the most." Rita fell quiet.

Glen must have sensed there was something else on her mind.

"And?"

"The check came in from Cliff's life insurance policy," Rita began.

Glen cut her off. "Rita, if you're thinking about paying company bills with that, let me stop you right there. No. You need that money."

He and Cliff were best friends. Was he being gallant? Or had Cliff confided in him about his financial maneuvers? Did he know how right he was? "We may not have a choice," she responded, "because people are counting on their paychecks."

He nodded, picked up the phone receiver and punched a four-digit extension. "Michelle, Glen here. Would you please join me in Rita's office? And bring the checking account balance and the list of current payables, including the payroll numbers."

Within minutes the office manager had joined them and passed out copies of the reports Glen had requested.

Glen was the first to speak. "Right off the bat, I'd like to take my salary off the list."

"Oh, Glen, that's not fair. You've more than earned your salary lately," Rita said.

"Please don't give it a second thought. I'm okay to wait until the pay period after we've gotten the LA check." Rita opened her mouth, but Glen held up his hand. "It's the least I can do for the company and Cliff."

"Thank you, Glen."

"I wish I could do that," Michelle blurted. Glen and Rita looked at her, surprised at the outburst. "Um, my boyfriend got laid off last week, and we really need my paycheck."

"There's no reason to apologize," Rita assured her. She picked up a pencil and took a breath. "Let's go through the accounts payable line-by-line and see what we can do." Rita checked the bank balance, scanned the invoice amounts and stopped abruptly at one particular entry. Her eyes bugged out in disbelief. "Okay. The payroll amount is higher than I thought it would be, but what's with the payroll taxes? That's huge! And that's due now? Wasn't money set aside for that?"

Michelle straightened in her chair. "We always meant to put those monies in a separate account, but every attempt was met with a new crisis. So every quarter Mr. Sterling somehow came up with it just in time to make the payments."

Rita thought about all the transfers out of their personal accounts. If she went back and checked withdrawal dates, they probably would correspond with the quarterly payroll reports

"The payments are due April 30th, and the government doesn't have a sense of humor when it comes to payroll issues," Michelle grimaced. "Penalties are substantial for both filing and paying after the due date."

"Why am I just now hearing about this?" Rita asked Michelle. "I would think an expense this large would have been worth mentioning at some point in the last two months, knowing we were making critical financial decisions."

"I had the money earmarked when we had to purchase a rack of high-end servers for the LA project," Michelle explained. "It was from a supplier we had never used before, and they demanded payment on delivery. Our credit line is maxed out. I had no choice." She paused and faced Rita squarely. "I apologize. I should have made you aware of the situation when it happened."

"Yes, that would have been the appropriate thing to do," Rita said, processing the information she was just given. Not that it would have made any difference, she thought, but she didn't like being blindsided. She penciled the math. "All right. There goes a big chunk out of cash reserves. Then, of course, there's payroll, which puts us in the red before we even consider anything else on this list."

"Let's work through it and come up with a number," Glen said.

Rita went back to her papers. "Rent. I'll call the leasing agent and let him know we'll be a little late. Utilities. We need to take care of those. Medical insurance. Wow. But, absolutely. Minimum payments on the corporate credit cards and credit line. I'll call the bank. 401k contributions. No choice." She punched numbers into her calculator. "Even if I can get a couple of these expenses postponed until we get the LA check, we're still short about $50,000. Am I doing that right?"

Glen and Michelle completed their calculations, looked at Rita and nodded.

The amount pushed her back into her chair. "Well, I have quite a tax bill of my own, but I could come up with maybe $20,000. That's still

$30,000 short. Where can we come up with that kind of money on such short notice?" Rita's thoughts returned to Cliff's IRA money that Lori said was sacred. Unbeknownst to her at the time, he had already tapped some of that before he passed away, which caused the majority of their tax liability. Because he didn't meet any of the exceptions for the early distribution penalty, the withdrawal was not only included in their income but also subject to a 10% penalty, which was like an additional tax. There was some left in the account, but she didn't want to touch it unless it was an absolute necessity. Unless they could come up with an alternative, the situation was fast approaching just that.

"I know of a venture capitalist who might be willing to put up some money," Glen volunteered. "But he's either going to want a high interest rate on a loan arrangement or SterTechCo shares."

Rita thought about that a moment before responding. "I don't want to incur any more debt if I can help it, and I certainly don't want to dilute the shares. I think it's important to keep SterTechCo in the family." The threesome fell silent for quite some time. Finally, Rita spoke. "There's one other option, but I'm not sure they'll go for it."

"What's that?" Glen asked.

"Let me do some checking," Rita said. "I'll give you a call before the close of business today. If that idea doesn't work, we'll reconvene for more brainstorming. Okay?" Glen and Michelle nodded. "Good. I'll be in touch later."

It was a long shot, but worth a try. She crossed her fingers as she picked up the phone.

Twenty-Six

The next few weeks were consumed with activity for the circle of friends. Marla drew, painted, assembled the items for her product, and went live on *eBay*. The first couple of days she stared at the computer screen expecting and praying for a sale to register, but none came. The following days she left the website up and checked it between household chores. Still nothing. Disappointment was beginning to set in. She needed a pep talk. The digital clock on the microwave displayed 8:30. She picked up the phone and called Lori's office.

"How's it going?" her friend asked.

"I wish I could say I'm flooded with orders and on my way to becoming rich and famous," Marla answered.

"Not going so well, huh?"

"Not a single order, Lori," Marla said. "I thought by now I'd have at least one."

Tax season had come to an end, so Ned's hours had returned to the nine-to-five routine, which meant his preoccupation with taxes had shifted to an obsession with her daily activities. Up to this point her answers had been evasive. It wasn't that she was keeping secrets from him necessarily – it was more along the lines of not having much to say.

Right now her business was sketches and art supplies wrapped in a dream. When the time was right, she'd tell him everything.

"Originally, you talked about doing a website. Did you ever do one?" Lori asked.

"No," Marla said. "My friend Vivian, who was going to do it, didn't have time, and I couldn't afford to pay anyone to do it. I thought I'd at least get traffic on *eBay* and maybe wouldn't need one."

"You need one," Lori said, as she searched through her client cards. "Not everybody's surfing *eBay* for merchandise. You've got to have a presence on the Internet, and a website is how you do that."

"Any ideas?

She plucked a card from the Rolodex. "As a matter of fact, I know a graphic artist who's just getting her business off the ground. She's looking for projects to put in her portfolio, so I think she'd give you a great deal."

"How great?" Marla asked.

"I'll talk with her, and between the two of us we'll work something out. She wanted me to do some financial planning for her. Maybe we could exchange services."

"Oh, Lori, I couldn't ask you to do that," Marla said.

"You didn't. I volunteered."

"That's very generous," Marla said. "I promise I'll pay you back."

"Don't worry about that," Lori assured her. "Say, what happened with HGTV? Did you ever hear back from them?"

"Oh, yeah." Marla let out a sigh. "Their advertising fees are in the big leagues. I can't see a time in the foreseeable future when I'd be able to afford them."

"Too bad," her friend said. "That website would have been a great place to show your product." Lori paused. "I was just thinking … have you thought about posting a *YouTube* demonstration of your product?"

Marla found it hard to hide her surprise. "No. There's so much cute and cool out there. Who would want to watch me *paint*?"

Her friend chuckled. "Actually, I've come across people demonstrating various painting techniques."

"Then you've got more time on your hands than I thought."

"What do you have to lose?" Lori asked. "Bob has a recorder, and I know how to post the videos."

Marla considered the suggestion. It would be a way to get her product out there, but then she thought about her appearance on video. They say the camera adds 20 pounds, and she already had at least 20 to shed. She did a quick mental visual and gasped.

Lori interrupted her reflective sidebar. "What do you think?"

"Oh, it sounds like a good idea, but I'm not sure about getting in front of the camera," Marla finally admitted.

"You'll be fine," Lori assured. "That's what's so great about these *YouTube* clips. The best ones are authentic, not rehearsed. Bob can work the camera. I posted a video of the girls playing soccer for the grandparents to watch. How about we get together tomorrow and see what happens? We'll shoot a few takes and decide."

Marla acquiesced. There was no telling Lori "no" when she'd made up her mind. "Okay, you win."

"Great. We'll see you about 10:00?"

"That'll work," Marla said.

"Say, have you talked with Jade or Rita lately," Lori asked.

"No. I was just about to ask you the same thing. Jade should be getting ready to move, and isn't SterTechCo approaching some sort of deadline?" The fact was she had been so busy with her business, the boys, and keeping Ned at bay that there had been little time left in the day.

"Do you have time to call Jade and find out if there's anything we can do for her? And I'll check in with Rita," Lori suggested.

"Can do," Marla said. "By the way, is everything okay with you? I think you freaked all of us out when you mentioned you and Bob were having problems."

"Oh, he's hanging in there. He falls off the wagon, so to speak, every now and then – buying when he should be selling online. But he's sold a few things and pretty much keeping to his allowance. I suppose I can't expect an about-face overnight." There's some optimism talking, she thought. The fact of the matter was their moment of financial truth was looming, and the enormity of the situation had been keeping her up at night. She didn't want to be a single parent. She didn't want to be single … period. But more importantly, she didn't want to wake up one day broke and out of time.

"It sounds like he's working at it. That's good." Marla paused. "So I'll see you tomorrow, and I'll call Jade and let you know if she needs anything. You'll do the same with Rita?"

Lori agreed, and the two friends clicked off.

~

"Are you okay? You're breathing hard," Marla asked Jade when she answered the phone.

"Just moving boxes, that's all." She had been doing little else for the last couple of days in preparation for the move. During the week off from work, she had managed to complete many of the solo projects – painting, caulking around windows and doors, power-washing the exterior, tiling and grouting. When Brian was available, they installed window treatments and finished the kitchen. During the last few weeks Jade had to force herself to keep moving through the exhaustion which had infiltrated every fiber of her body. Nightly hot baths and regular doses of aspirin had become the daily protocol for aching muscles with de minimus results, but the end was in sight.

"Can we help you with anything?" Marla asked.

"Thanks, but I've got a large truck and two young, strong and inexpensive guys coming tomorrow," Jade answered. "No sense risking the chance of anybody I know getting hurt because they're doing something they're not used to doing."

"So you've closed on the house already?"

"It's this afternoon at one," Jade answered.

"Well, you better get going," Marla suggested. "It's 12:45."

Jade's eyes darted to the wall clock. "Ohmigod. Thanks. Talk to you later." She clicked off, snatched the car keys from the counter and sprinted to her car.

Ten minutes later she waved as she passed Mark's receptionist on her way down the hall toward the conference room. The group simultaneously checked the time as Jade dashed in the door and slid into an empty chair. "Sorry. I think I made every red light."

Mark smiled at Jade and began. "First, I'll need a driver's license from each of you so I can complete my notary book." The group complied, and he made the appropriate entries and returned the licenses. Then Mark slid a stack of documents in front of Jade and another set in front of the Atwoods. "We'll go through each of these and I'll show you where you need to sign," Mark continued. With that he announced the title of each document, explained the gist of the pages of legalese and pointed to the signature lines. Minutes later they were done, and Mark excused himself to get copies made.

Jade turned to the Atwoods. "I just want to thank you again for allowing me to purchase your house and for working with me on the financing. I really appreciate it. And please feel free to come by any time."

Frank and Amelia nodded. Tony spoke. "You're welcome, and thanks for the invite."

"Oh, well, of course you'll be by to pick up the stuff in the carriage house and the furniture in the apartment." Her tone was matter-of-fact.

The Atwoods looked at one another. "I don't want any of that junk. You two can have it," Amelia said to her brothers.

"I haven't been in the carriage house for years," Frank added. "As far as I can remember, there was nothing but old hardware and whatever else Dad scavenged from around the neighborhood. I doubt there's anything in there I'd be interested in."

"Do you want to look?" Tony asked him.

"No. It's all yours."

Tony turned to Jade. "Then I guess it's all yours. Well, that is, if you want it."

Jade grimaced. The thought of another project of that magnitude made her already exhausted body scream for mercy.

"Pardon me," Tony continued. "I don't mean to make it sound as though we're dumping this on you. If you want us to clean the place out, let me know, and I'll take care of it. A buddy of mine does hauling for me from time to time."

"Thanks for all of that," Jade said. "Right now the last thing I want to do is pick up another box, but we'll see how I feel a few weeks or months from now."

"There's no expiration date on the offer," Tony assured her.

Mark returned to the conference room and passed out a stapled stack of papers to each. "Congratulations, everybody," he said, as he began to shake hands around the room. "I'm glad this arrangement worked out for all of us."

The group agreed while the hand-shaking made the rounds. Jade reiterated the invitation to the Atwoods. "I mean it now. You're welcome to come by any time."

Tony tipped his Stetson. "Thank you. That's very kind."

~

Lori punched in Rita's office number, and Carmen answered. "Is she in?"

"Yes, but she closed the door and asked that I hold all calls."

"Is everything okay?"

Carmen went on. "It's been kinda weird around here today. I don't know what's going on."

"I'm on my way," Lori told her and hung up.

Within the hour Lori walked into Carmen's office and glanced at Rita's door. "Is anybody with her?"

Carmen shook her head.

Lori lightly rapped on the door, gently turned the knob and peeked in. Rita was sitting behind the desk with her eyes closed. "Rita, it's Lori."

With that she took a deep breath and rose from her chair. "Oh, come in." She straightened her blouse into her skirt and met Lori halfway across the room with a hug. "To what do I owe the pleasure of a visit during a work day?"

"When I called, Carmen said you didn't want to be interrupted. I just wanted to make sure you were okay," Lori said.

Rita put her arm around Lori's waist, and the two strolled toward the couch. "We made the deadline," Rita announced.

"That's great," Lori said. "So why the long face?"

Rita nestled up against the sofa's arm rest and propped up her elbow. Lori pulled a nearby upholstered chair close to the couch, sat down and leaned in toward her friend. "We're going to run out of money before we get paid on the project," Rita answered, stroking her deep frown lines as though she could rub them away. "We'll make payroll, and I got some of our creditors to wait, but we're short $30,000."

"Doesn't SterTechCo have a line of credit for just such cash flow situations?" Lori asked.

"Tapped out."

"Have you asked them if they'd consider increasing it?"

"Yes, and the answer is 'no'," Rita said. "Apparently the numbers weren't all that great last year."

"I see."

Rita looked at her friend. "I'm going to take it out of Cliff's IRA." She held up her hand. "I know how you feel about that, but I'm afraid I have no other choice. I've already called them and the paperwork is on my desk."

"Although," Lori began, "as the surviving spouse, if you reinvest the money in *your* IRA within sixty days of receiving the withdrawal, the distribution is not taxable."

Rita pondered the information for a moment. "And if I don't meet the sixty-day deadline?"

"Then whatever you don't reinvest will be included in your income for the current year," Lori explained.

"Really?" Rita perked up. "Then it's settled. That's what I'll do."

"There's one small caveat," Lori began. "They automatically withhold 20% for taxes, so you'll have to pay that back too, bringing the total to $36,000. Of course when you file your tax returns next year, you'll get credit for the $6,000 they withheld, and you may get some of that back."

"And if I don't pay it back?" Rita asked.

"Whatever you don't pay back will be included in your income, and the penalty will apply," Lori explained.

"Good to know. Thanks," Rita said and smiled. "I think I'm going to wait a little while longer. We could still get the check in time."

Lori checked her watch. "Say, I've got to go pick up the girls from school. Want to tag along?"

Rita jumped off the couch. "I'd love to. I feel so much better now. I'll call Glen on the way and let him in on the game plan."

Twenty-Seven

Jade's life was finally beginning to feel normal again, mostly thanks to Brian. Not only had he worked tirelessly to finish all the projects at the other house, he'd coordinated the movers so she could unpack as boxes were unloaded at the Atwood house. Since the move, he had worked with her to rebuild and paint the front porch, replace the steps leading to the apartment over the carriage house, trim the hedge and power-wash the house. The list of future projects at her new home grew by the day, but at least the place was safe and clean.

She was becoming quite fond of Brian. Over the last few months they had eaten together almost every night and never seemed to run out of things to talk about. There had been accidental touching while fixing this or that, followed by blushing and stuttering awkwardness on both sides. She wasn't sure what all that meant. She wasn't good at boy/girl signals. In fact, she would have missed having her first boyfriend in high school if he hadn't had too much to drink one night and professed his undying love for her. Maybe there wasn't anything more to her relationship with Brian than enjoying each other's company. Oh hell. This is why she wasn't in a relationship.

Jade checked her watch. The open house guests would be arriving soon. She was excited to get together with her friends. They all had been so busy the last couple of weeks that they had no time to catch up. She lit candles and straightened the towels in the bathroom, double-checked the master for stray shoes, arranged plates, cups and napkins on the dining table and was headed back to the kitchen when the doorbell rang.

"Hi, Marla." Jade hugged her. "Come in."

"Thank you." Just inside the front door Marla stumbled to a stop and pivoted on her heel. The house had a way of stopping people in their tracks. "It's beautiful. I love the carved cornice and huge windows."

"Me, too." Jade let her friend check out the rest of the room's details before grabbing her hand. "Let me give you the tour." The two snaked through the house, ending up peering out the window of the back door. "And there's the carriage house and the apartment above that, but I haven't had a chance to touch either one of them yet."

"I'd love to see them anyway, if you don't mind," Marla said. "You know how I like to poke around." With that the two stepped out of the house and across the yard to the massive carriage house doors. Jade flipped the hinge and yanked on the wooden door, exposing the dust-laden contents.

"Boy, that's a lot of stuff," Marla remarked as her eyes scanned the interior. "You say, you don't know what's in here?"

"Tony told me it's mostly odds and ends his dad scavenged from around the neighborhood on his daily walks. I figure I'll get around to it one of these days."

"You let me know if you need any help," Marla volunteered. "It'd be like a treasure hunt."

"I'm not sure about the 'treasure' part, but I'll call you. Let's go upstairs." Jade closed up the garage, and the two made their way to the apartment.

"It needs some updating, but it'd be perfect for a college student."

Jade agreed as they surveyed the small efficiency. The hardwood floor peeked through the threadbare carpet, and stuffing popped through the side chair and single mattress. The two-burner stove and small sink cabinet nestled in the corner looked to be in good shape. With a few new pieces of furniture and a good scrubbing, it would be ready for a tenant.

"We'd better get back to the house. I still have a few things to do before everybody else gets here," Jade said.

"What can I do?" Marla volunteered when they got back to the kitchen.

"You can arrange the veggies on the tray while I put the meatballs in the warming dish." The two went to work. "So what have you been up to? How's the business going?"

Marla swirled around to face her friend. "Ohmigod!" Her face flushed, and her breathing hastened. "Fantastic! Beyond my wildest dreams!"

"Tell me! Tell me!"

"Well, at first I put it up on *eBay* and nothing. Like for a week. So I called Lori, and she suggested I do a *YouTube* video and a website. I thought the whole *YouTube* thing was silly, but it worked! I've gotten orders like you wouldn't believe. I hired my friend Rachel to help with the shipping, and I'm already working on some new designs."

"That's fantastic!" Jade gushed. "What does Ned have to say about all that?"

"I had kept it under wraps for quite a while. When I finally told him, he was shocked. He couldn't believe any of it – how I came up with the idea, how I took it to market, how I've handled the business part of it." She paused and giggled into her hand. "To be honest, I've been a little surprised, too. I never thought of myself as an entrepreneur or business person. If it hadn't been for that conversation we had about me thinking outside the career box and for all the encouragement from you guys, I'm not sure I would have taken the chance."

"I'm so happy for you!" Jade said.

"And then there's the whole money conversation I had with Ned," Marla continued. "If it hadn't been for our workshops, I may never have found out what was going on with our finances."

Jade transferred the cooked meatballs into the chaffing dish, set it in its metal holder and transported it to the table before lighting the Bunsen burner and the candles in the centerpiece. As she returned to the kitchen, she asked, "So how's that going? Are you working on the finances together?"

Marla had trimmed and placed the last of the cauliflower in the lazy Susan and poured the ranch dressing into the center dish. "That and more."

Jade raised her eyebrows. "Really?"

Marla's cheeks pinkened. "I mean, we go grocery shopping together. We're learning to cook as a family. Eating dinner at home is sure saving us a lot, and it's so much healthier. I've lost ten pounds already and Ned, twenty. Anyway, we're talking like we did when we were dating. Somewhere he got the notion – probably from his father – that the family's total financial well-being rested on the man's shoulders, which was a huge burden. It's no wonder when he lost everything, he was devastated. I'm sorry the money's gone, but not sorry it happened. Does that make sense?"

"Totally," Jade said. "Now you're a team, which may never have happened otherwise."

Marla responded with a reflective nod. "By the way, have you rented your house yet?"

Jade selected a couple of bottles of wine from the cupboard and turned to answer her friend. "That was craziest thing. I had a few calls and a few lookers from the advertising I did at the hospital and on *craigslist*, but no takers. And I'd been so busy with getting all the work done around there that I hadn't had time to put up a 'for rent' sign. Then, on moving day, my neighbor across the street came over and asked what was going on. When I told her I was going to rent my place, she said her nephew was getting married, and they were looking for something in the neighborhood. She made a call, and by that afternoon I had a signed lease. I couldn't believe it!"

"Sounds like we have a lot to celebrate!" Marla said. "And Ned is going to pick me up, so I'm going to have a glass of wine."

Still holding a bottle in each hand, Jade presented one, then the other. "Red or white?"

"Red," her friend answered. "The perfect compliment to those famous meatballs of yours."

When the doorbell rang, Jade said to Marla, "If you'll get that, I'll get this bottle open."

"Will do," she said as she hurried toward the door.

~

Lori rapped on the front door of Rita's house and peeked through the side window. "Yoo-hoo."

Her friend was on the couch sitting upright with her legs tucked tightly underneath and her head resting on the side cushion.

"Rita."

Rita's eyes popped open, and she waved. She slowly unfolded her body, padded toward the door, and greeted Lori with a hug.

Lori gave her the once over. "Did you forget we were going to Jade's open house today?"

Rita gently shook her head, closed the door behind Lori and yawned. "No. I guess time just got away from me. Give me a moment. I'll change."

"Is everything okay?" Lori followed her friend into the bedroom.

"Everything is good," Rita answered, shimmying out of the yoga pants and pulling the large T-shirt over her head.

"What's been going on?" Lori took a seat on the edge of the unmade king-size bed as Rita shuffled into the walk-in closet.

Lori could hear Rita sliding hangers across the wooden rod before reappearing with a v-neck, sleeveless top and matching capri's. "Well, I was all set to withdraw the $30,000 from Cliff's IRA like we talked about when the darndest thing happened." She removed the items from their hangers and faced her friend. "Brian and Christine loaned SterTechCo their life insurance money from Cliff."

"You're kidding! How did that happened?"

Rita began to put on her pants. "Brian called to check on me and to find out how things were going at SterTechCo. I guess we've both been quite busy and haven't been in touch much. Anyway, when I told him where we were with everything, he called his sister, and they showed up within hours with checks in hand."

"I can't believe they did that," Lori said.

Now dressed, Rita sat down next to her friend. "Me, either. But I guess loyalty to their father's company was deeper than any of us realized. When push came to shove, they couldn't stand by and let SterTechCo close down when they could do something to stop it."

"So the company will be okay moving forward?" Lori asked.

"For a while, I think. The LA check is quite substantial and should hold us over. Plus, a couple of smaller projects are close to being finished, which will bring in some additional revenue."

Lori heaved a huge sigh. "Boy, I bet that's a load off your mind."

Rita nodded, then looked away. A tear escaped down her cheek.

"What's all that about?" Lori wrapped her arm around Rita's shoulder.

The tears streamed down her face. "Oh, I don't know. Probably the last two months catching up with me. Being at SterTechCo, working in Cliff's office, the pressure of the deadline." Rita sobbed. "And I miss Cliff so much."

"I know." Lori plucked a tissue from the box on the night stand and handed it to Rita.

Rita dabbed her eyes. "And it's like I'm in the same place I was two months ago. I still don't know what to do or where I belong. Maybe I should go back to my old job at the station."

Lori waited while Rita blew and blotted through three more tissues before speaking. "That's not a decision you need to make today. Take some time to figure out where you want to go from here. The company is solvent for now and the insurance money will get you by for a few more months."

"You're right." Rita acquiesced to another sniffle.

The two friends sat quietly for a moment. Then Lori pulled herself up and Rita along with her. "Before you get all introspective, we have a party to go to. Are you ready?"

"I'm probably a sight. Let me check my makeup and hair," she answered and headed toward the vanity area in the master bath.

Lori followed and leaned against the wall facing the mirror. "I can't wait to see this house of Jade's."

"Me, either." Rita squeezed the last of her tears from her lashes, applied mascara, blushed her cheeks and brushed her hair.

"You know," Lori started. "Maybe Jade's got something." Rita's look turned quizzical. "Falling in love with houses sure seems a lot less complicated than falling in love with men."

"You're just saying that because of what's going on with you and Bob." Rita sprayed and scrunched her hair to add volume.

"Maybe."

"I think that as much as Jade likes houses, if the right person came along, she could be persuaded to redirect that passion," Rita said.

"I hope for both their sakes he shows up soon. A few more houses, and she'll be too busy for anyone or anything else in her life."

Rita examined herself in the mirror. "There. I'm as ready as I'm going to be."

Lori looked at her friend. The last few months had shed a few pounds from her already slender frame, but she was as stunning as ever. "I don't know about you, but I'm starving."

"Now that you mention it, I could use some of Jade's special munchies."

"Then let's get going before they're all gone," Lori said, grabbing Rita's hand.

Be on the lookout for the next installment of The Bread & Butter Chronicles, Dough Rising, *in which Rita, Marla, Jade, and Lori face new personal and financial challenges.*

In the meantime, please visit starrcochran.com and let her know what financial topics you'd like to see addressed in future books. Thank you.

Appendix

What to Do When
Your Spouse Dies

Your emotions are running deep, and all you want to do is grieve. Yet there are decisions to be made; financial matters to tend to. Where do you begin?

First of all, take a breath. Little can be done until you receive the death certificate, which can take weeks, and many issues are not urgent. In fact, some areas are best postponed and dealt with when emotions are less raw. (See the section on the next page entitled "**Things you can put off until later.**")

Do you have a trusted friend or family member who could help you? Details of the tasks involved can be overwhelming. Emotions can cloud your ability to make decisions, and the sheer activity of settling the estate can be physically challenging. An extra pair of eyes and hands can bring a welcomed peace of mind.

Gather important papers.
- *Death certificate.* Obtain at least five certified copies, which are provided by the funeral director. Some companies want certified copies; others are satisfied with regular copies.
- *Insurance policies.*
- *Marriage certificate.* Some companies will ask for a copy of this document.
- *Military discharge papers.* If you cannot locate these, write to:

> Department of Defense
> National Personnel Record Center
> 9700 Page Blvd.
> St. Louis, MO 63132

- *Will and/or Trust.* Depending upon the complexity of these documents, you may want to solicit the assistance of an attorney to assure the provisions are properly executed.

- *List of current assets and liabilities.* If you do not have a current list, you will need to compile one. This list will include assets from brokerage and bank accounts, annuities, mutual funds, retirement accounts, real estate held for investment purposes as well as the value of your home and personal property such as vehicles, jewelry, collectibles, etc. (A sample of one is available in this Appendix under **Balance Sheet.**)
- *Children's birth certificates and Social Security numbers.* If you have dependent children, you will need this information to apply for Social Security benefits.

Apply for benefits. Make copies of everything you send. Documents can get lost or misplaced. Also, set up some sort of tracking system for the paperwork. (One is available in this Appendix under **Estate Paperwork Tracking Form.**)

- *Insurance proceeds.* Contact your local agents if possible. Otherwise, get in touch with the company. Find out what paperwork is necessary to collect benefits from life insurance and accidental death policies, mortgage insurance policies, credit card protection policies, and from employer-provided policies.
- *Social Security benefits.* If your spouse paid into Social Security, you may be entitled to several benefits.
  - One-time death benefit of around $250 towards burial expenses. Your local Social Security office or funeral director can assist with the paperwork.
  - Survivor's benefits for you or children. You may be eligible for survivor's benefits if:
    - You are over 60 years old;
    - You are a disabled widow under 50 years old; or

- You care for dependent children under 16 or disabled.

Contact your local Social Security Administration office, call 800-772-1213 or check online at *www.ssa.gov.*

- *Veteran burial benefit.* Survivors of veterans are eligible to receive a lump-sum payment of $300 for burial expenses and a plot interment allowance of $300. (Burial in a national cemetery is free to a veteran, his or her spouse, and dependent children.) Veterans are also eligible for a headstone or grave marker at no charge. The funeral director can help you apply for these benefits, or you can contact the regional Department of Veterans Affairs office.
- *Employee benefits.* If your spouse was employed at the time of death, there may be benefits such as:
  - Accumulated sick and/or vacation leave.
  - Life, health, accident insurance benefits.
  - Death benefits associated with your spouse's professional organization or union.
  - Pension plan. (See information below regarding retirement accounts.)
  - Workman's compensation benefits if your spouse's death was work-related.

Begin to settle the estate. If your spouse had a will and you were designated as the personal representative or executor of the estate, the estate may have to be probated. (Check your state's law for its minimum estate amount.) This process includes:
  - Filing a petition with the court after death, along with a fee for the probate process.
  - Proving that the will is valid.
  - Informing creditors, heirs and beneficiaries.
  - Disposing of the estate in accordance with the will.

If there is no will, the court will appoint a personal representative (usually the surviving spouse), and the estate will be distributed according to state law.

Assets held jointly with someone else are transferred to the surviving owner outside of probate and outside of the will. Insurance proceeds and retirement accounts also pass to the beneficiary outside of probate.

Evaluate short-term income and expenses. Your income and expenses have just changed. A Cash Income & Expenditures Statement can give you an idea where you stand financially so you can determine what adjustments need to be made in the short-term to meet your monthly obligations. (A sample is available in this Appendix.)

Change ownership and update beneficiaries.
- *Bank and investment accounts.*
- *Your life insurance policies.*
- *Automobiles.*
- *Annuities and retirement accounts, including employer retirement plans and IRAs.* Depending upon the type of retirement account, decisions in this area can be complex. It is recommended that you consult with a professional advisor, such as a Certified Financial Planner™ or CPA or Enrolled Agent to explain the short- and long-term implications of the various distribution options.
- *Credit cards.* Cards issued in the name of the deceased spouse only should be cancelled. For those credit cards held in both of your names, notify the institution that your spouse is deceased and to list the card in your name only.

Ask for professional help. There's nothing wrong with asking for help from a professional advisor. In fact, their expertise can save you time and perhaps costly mistakes.

Things you can put off until later. What a difference a year makes. These are noncritical, more emotionally driven decisions that can wait.
- Selling your possessions or giving them away.

- Moving.
- Buying things.
- Giving money away or makings loans to others.
- Investing.
- Evaluating insurance needs.
- Estate planning.
- Retirement planning.

There are few more challenging times in life than dealing with the death of a spouse. However, following these steps to get your financial affairs in order, and surrounding yourself with family and friends can make the process less overwhelming.

Estate Paperwork Tracking Table

Company Address Phone #	Contact Person	Benefit/Name Change	Paperwork Requested/ Date	Paperwork Received/Date	Paperwork Sent/Date	Resolution

Willing to Transfer – or Not

The Use of Wills, Trusts, Contracts and Titling to Transfer Assets

What's a living trust? Do you need a trust? What's a living will? What's the difference between a will and a living will? Do you need a will? Or a living will? What's a TOD account? POD account?

A living trust is a revocable trust established during your lifetime and allows the trustee virtually complete control over the assets. Should you become incapacitated or disabled, the trust is in place to manage your financial affairs. At death, the assets are distributed and managed according to the trust document under the supervision of a successor trustee. A will is a legal document that allows you to distribute your property to those you choose, and if you have minor children, the will also gives you the opportunity to nominate a guardian. A living will is a document that outlines your medical wishes in the event you are unable to speak for yourself, such as what measures you would like to be taken to keep you alive. TOD (Transfer on Death) and POD (Payable on Death) are types of account titling which can enable you to maintain control of the account yet allow for the account to pass to the person(s) named upon your death.

Because estate planning is governed by state law, the differences among the states are as diverse as they are. Even laws in community property states vary significantly. So it is a good idea to know your options based on your state's law. Having said that, the area of transferring assets at time of death doesn't have to be overwhelming, and the answers to a few simple questions can guide you through the decision-making process.

Would you consider yourself a do-it-yourselfer or someone who would rather rely on the advice of others? If you like to do things yourself, you will probably be comfortable doing the necessary research to determine which route will best suit your needs – a trust, a will, titling, or a combination – and then putting your choices into place. On the other hand, if you're more comfortable with a professional, an attorney in your area specializing in estate planning can advise you as to which method would best suit your situation.

Would you consider yourself a technical person or an emotional person? If you think of yourself as being more emotional than technical, you would probably be best served by establishing a trust. Trusts allow you to take care of everything, including the financial affairs of your family after your death. If you lean toward the technical side, a will, titling and beneficiary designations might be the way to go.

Are you a private person or would you mind if your affairs were public knowledge? If you consider yourself a private person, a trust gives you that privacy plus expediency. A will is public record, and it allows a certain number of months for creditors to come forward with claims, which could delay settling the estate. As mentioned earlier, assets in a trust are easily transferred and maintained because the entity lives on after death.

Do you have minor children? If you do, it is recommended you name a guardian in your will and establish a trust where your assets would be placed after your death for the benefit of your children. You will also have to name a trustee for that trust, which can be someone other than your children's guardian.

> This area is particularly important and deserves an example. Let's say you have two children and two sets of loving grandparents who would be equally qualified to care for the children. Without a guardian provision the courts could decide to split custody of the children between the grandparents, which may not be in the best interest of the children or conform to your wishes.

Regardless of which estate planning method(s) you choose, do something. If an individual has no will, or if the will is invalid, or if the will has been revoked, then that person has died "intestate." Some of the disadvantages to this lack of estate planning are:

• The laws of the state will determine who will receive the

property.
- A guardian is named by the court.
- The court appoints the personal representative, who may charge more for administrating the estate than a family member.
- For larger estates tax saving opportunities will be lost.

If your estate needs are straightforward, there are will kits available online as well as at local book and office supply stores. Check with your state's bar association online for a list of local attorneys who specialize in estate matters, then call for an estimate. As with the other aspects of your financial life, the more complicated your situation, the more sophisticated the planning options. If your estate needs go beyond straightforward, or if the process is outside your comfort zone, contact an attorney.

Cash Income & Expenditures Statement

		Per Month		**Per Year**
Your Income	Take home wages			
	Interest and dividends			
	Pensions and Social Security			
	Rental income			
	Other income			
	Total income			
Your Ex-penses	House payment/rent (35%)			
	Debt service (10%)			
	Credit card #1			
	Credit card #2			
	Credit card #3			
	Transportation (15%)			
	Car loan/lease #1			
	Car loan/lease #2			
	Gasoline			
	Maintenance			
	Insurance			
	Registration			
	Savings (10%)			

Cash Income & Expenditures Statement (Cont'd)

	Everything else (30%)			
	Groceries			
	Dining out			
	Child care/ tuition			
	Clothing			
	Utilities (water/ gas/electric/phone)			
	Cell phone			
	Cable			
	Entertainment			
	Homeowner association dues			
	Personal care			
	Other			
	Other			
	Total expenses			
Total Income				
(minus) Total Expenses				
Available for additional savings/ investments				

(This form is also available on *starrcochran.com*.)

Options – And the Trading of Them

An option is a contract that gives the buyer the option, but not the obligation, to buy or sell an investment, such as a stock, at a certain price and on or before a certain date. And the buyer pays a price for the option.

The easiest example of how options work is with real estate. Let's say that you find a house, but you won't have the money to purchase it for six months. You enter into a contract with the owner that gives you the option to purchase the house for $100,000; for that option you pay the owner $1,000. Two months later it might be discovered that the scribblings on the wall belong to Elvis and the house is now worth $1 million. The seller is obligated to sell you the house for $100,000. In the end you could net $899,000 from the transaction ($1,000,000 minus $100,000 minus $1,000). On the other hand, it could work out instead that a few months later the support beams give way, causing the house to slide down the hillside and come to rest on the highway below. In this case you would let the option expire and be out the $1,000.

With securities, option trading is more speculative and therefore riskier. You must guess correctly whether a stock is going to go up or down, when that's going to happen, and the price of the stock. One of the appealing aspects of option trading is that you don't necessarily have to own the stock, which means for very little money (the price of the option) you can control a block of stock. A small movement in the stock price could mean a large payoff – or a financial tsunami.

Options can be an excellent risk management tool to protect investments and a way to make substantial profits with minimal money upfront, but like any other strategy, without proper research, knowledge and monitoring, they can be hazardous to your financial health – as Ned found out.

The goal here is to give the definition of options, a brief description how they work, and a word of caution. Option trading is complex, and it's not for everyone. Ned thought he was ready for option trading after having traded stocks for a while and attending a workshop that sold trading software. He wasn't. He didn't practice long enough with imaginary money before making trades with real money. He didn't study the markets long enough, didn't watch his positions closely enough. He had a job with long hours and a family. Maybe he thought it would be as easy for him as it was for the workshop facilitator who only spent a couple of hours a day on the computer making trades. It wasn't.

There are many ways to make money. Trading options is one of them. Is it right for you? Only you can answer that. To learn more go to one of the discount brokerage firm websites such as *Schwab.com* or *TDAmeritrade.com* and check out their option trading tools and education.

Balance Sheet

Assets

Cash and Savings
Cash and checking accounts
Savings accounts
Certificates of deposit
U.S. savings bonds
Money market accounts
Other
Total Cash and Savings

Investment Assets
Stocks
Bonds
Mutual funds
Government securities
Employee stock options
Cash value of life insurance
Surrender value of annuities
Income-producing real estate
Total Investment Assets

Retirement Assets
Pension or profit sharing plans
IRA's/Keogh accounts
Employee savings plans, 401K's
Other
Total Retirement Assets

Non-Income Earning Assets
Home (market value)
Other non-income real estate
Furniture and equipment
Autos (market value)
Recreational vehicle, boat, etc
Collectibles
Jewelry
Other
Total Non-Income Earning Assets

Total Assets

Liabilities

Home mortgage
Other mortgages or notes
Car loans

Credit cards and charge accounts

Other loans

Taxes not withheld
Past due rent, interest
Amount borrowed on life insurance

Miscellaneous liabilities

Total Liabilities

Net Worth
   (assets minus liabilities)

(This form is also available on *starrcochran.com*.)

How to Increase Your Cash Flow Bottom Line

Could you relate to how Jade, Marla, Rita and Lori felt about their cash flow situations? Too much month left at the end of the money? Don't be discouraged. Get out your pencil and calculator, and let's see what you can do.

Income. What can you do to increase your income? Could you teach a class? Speak at a workshop or conference? Write an article for a professional publication, hobby magazine or local newspaper? Do you have a talent or hobby that could translate into a business? What are you already doing that you can charge for? Are there things around the house you could sell?

I have a friend who is an admin assistant by day and a seamstress by night. She contracted with a drycleaners for small mending jobs. The arrangement is a win-win situation. They get excellent work done at a reasonable price; she earns extra money in her spare time.

No need to focus on just one money-making idea. There are plenty of activities which can be performed simultaneously to maximize income production.

Expenses. Like Lori explained to her friends, depending on your financial situation, every expense can be reduced or eliminated – from housing to a cup of coffee. Critique each expense by asking yourself these questions:

> Do I need to spend this amount on this item?
> How can I lower this amount?
> Can I get rid of this expense all together?

There is no right or wrong answer, no perfect solution. The important thing is to work with these two sides of money flow to come up with the combination that's going to meet your goals and dreams.

Starr's Fifty Favorite Money-Saving Ideas

These are my favorites. They're easy, simple, and many have other benefits besides saving money.

1. **Swap stuff**. Especially stuff you only use periodically like painting materials.

2. **Turn off the television**. Save electricity; avoid enticing ads to buy stuff; spend quality time with your family and friends.

3. **Invite friends over instead of going out**. Rotate houses; do potluck.

4. **Use fewer paper towels**. Pick up a rag or an old towel to mop up the latest spill. Also, opt for cloth napkins instead of paper.

5. **Go generic.** You might be surprised how good the store brands are for many groceries.

6. **Plan your meals around what's on sale this week**. Your ingredients are fresh, and you can cut down on freezer waste.

7. **Organize your closets**. It's amazing what lurks in closets. You may find items you didn't know you had that can be used again, sold, or passed on to someone who could use them.

8. **Watch the water**. Turn off the water while brushing your teeth, shaving or doing dishes. Adjust the water flow under the sink. When washing vegetables, put some cool water in the sink and do them there (the dirt sinks to the bottom). Consider a drip irrigation system for your yard. Shower with a friend.

9. **Skip the bottled water.** Buy a refillable water bottle and fill from home by using a water filtration device.

10. **Use it up, wear it out, make it do, or do without.**

11. **Quit smoking.**

12. **Use half the dishwasher soap.** Try different cycles to see if your dishes get just as clean without running the full cycle, and skip the drying cycle.

13. **Bank online.** It's safe, easy, and it saves the postage.

14. **Use the library.** You can borrow books, CDs and DVDs, and you can read newspapers and magazines there.

15. **Get the cash back.** Use credit cards that offer cash back or other incentives.

16. **Clean with white vinegar and shampoo.** Use vinegar and water for floors and countertops; shampoo on tubs and tiles. Vinegar combined with baking soda also makes a great drain cleaner. Pour baking soda down the drain; follow with the vinegar until you don't see bubbles any more.

17. **Give yourself a buy time out.** Before purchasing an unnecessary item, give yourself a 30-day time out. It's amazing how unimportant the purchase seems a month later.

18. **Buy in bulk.** If the amount is too much for you, share with a friend.

19. **Stock up on sale.** Nonperishables have a long shelf life. Take advantage of those items when they're on sale.

20. **Clip coupons.** And check for coupons online, too.

21. **Bundle up.** Combine your cable, Internet and telephone service.

22. **Prepare meals at home.** Get an easy-to-use cookbook and start cooking. You'll find making your meals at home is easier than you think, cheaper and healthier.

23. **Get rid of Private Mortgage Insurance**. If you put less than 20% down on your home, you're probably paying PMI. Once the equity in your home is at least 20%, contact your mortgage company about removing the PMI.

24. **Look for rebates and send them in.** They are available on a variety of products, so look for them when shopping.

25. **Take your lunch to work**. As often as possible.

26. **Keep your car longer.**

27. **Get rid of your home phone.** If you're not comfortable with relying solely on your cell phone, consider reducing the services to the minimum.

28. **Scale back on the gift giving.** Set limits on gift giving within your circle of family and friends.

29. **Use gifts bags instead of wrapping paper when possible**. They're recyclable.

30. **Drink less alcohol.** It costs money and adds calories.

31. **Buy online.** Compare prices while taking into account postage, sales tax and minimum orders.

32. **Take advantage of your employer's 401k matches**. Do whatever you can to take advantage of those matches.

33. **Use your company's flex spending accounts.** Contributions, which come out pre-tax, pay for certain medical, dental and child care expenses. The deductibility of these expenses can be limited, so paying for them "off the top" of your income can't be beat.

34. **Check out your cable service.** You may find that you're paying for channels you're not watching.

35. **Refinance your mortgage.** If you can reduce your interest rate by at least one percentage point, it's often beneficial to

refinance. Ask about costs, including points. Check with your current mortgage holder. Oftentimes they'll work with you to keep your business.

36.   **Don't spend big money entertaining your kids.** Most children, especially younger ones, can be entertained quite cheaply. Be creative. Use items around the house to make carnival games, build a fort, put on a puppet show. Consider a sandbox in the back yard. Go to the park.

37.   **Turn off and unplug.** Flip the switch when you leave the room and unplug electrical devices when not in use.

38.   **Go shopping full and with a list in hand.** You'll spend less at the grocery store on a full stomach and armed with a list that you stick to.

39.   **Sign up for reward cards**. Ask the establishments you frequent if they have a reward card. Also, check to see if you can sign up at their website for discount coupons.

40.   **Swap books, music, and DVDs.** You can do this among friends and family, over the Internet or at your local used book store.

41.   **Combine errands**. You can save time and fuel by combining errands.

42.   **Make gifts or give a gift of service.** It truly is the thought that counts. Create simple gifts with a handwritten note from the heart or volunteer to perform a service such as babysitting, walking the dog or cleaning up the yard.

43.   **Stay away from convenience stores as much as possible.** Items there are generally more expensive.

44.   **Use a crock pot**. It's probably the best idea for reducing cooking costs for the busy family. Put the ingredients in the crock in the morning, turn it on *simmer*, and dinner is ready

when you get home.

45. **Buy a smaller house.** The larger the home, the larger everything – insurance, utilities, maintenance costs. Plus it takes more time to clean it and to do the yard work.

46. **Have a clothes swap party**. Gather a group of friends who are about the same size and swap clothes and shoes.

47. **Check your cell phone minutes**. Are you going over your minutes every month? Maybe not using all your minutes? A few changes in your plan could save you every month.

48. **Store food properly.** Use Debbie Myer's *green produce bags*. Invest in a vacuum-packing food saver system.

49. **Look for your grocery store's in-store specials and discount items**. In the perishable sections of the store such as meat, produce and bakery, you may find an area which contains discounted items that are close to their expiration date.

50. **Talk with your loved ones about what your dreams are.** This may not sound like a money-saving idea, but if you spend time talking about your dreams and get the family on board, there is a better chance everyone will work together to make those dreams come true.

Getting From At-Home to On-the-Job

Returning to the workforce after an absence to raise a family can often be challenging, to say the least. Much like Marla in Starr Cochran's novel, you may not know where to begin. Here are a few suggestions to get you started.

Identify Your Skill Sets. What are your skill sets? Sit down and make a list for yourself. What do you do well in your everyday life? Okay, now, which abilities are transferable to workplace occupations, and specifically, the occupations you're interested in? These marketable skills may include multi-tasking, prioritizing, decision-making, time management and many other strengths that you apply in your home life and can transfer to the office or other environment where you might be able to earn your daily bread.

Now think beyond your life at home. Which skill sets did you apply in your volunteer jobs in your kids' schools or other organizations? Might these abilities include leadership, coaching, mentoring, event coordination or others? These talents may well be desired by potential employers.

And you can even go back a way to look for your proficiencies. What did you learn in your college years? These skills may include writing reports/papers, conducting research, team work if you had any group projects, and others. (Check out the *career self-assessment tools* at *www.bluestarcareers.com*.)

Identify Professional Areas of Interest. Once you have identified your skills and your accomplishments, you can explore what you want to do professionally. First, what do you dream that you might do? What are you passionate about? What would get you out of bed in the morning, excited to tackle every work day? You may already know what you want to do, what you love to do, but perhaps you aren't allowing yourself to dream, or you have a couple of "nay-sayers" in your life. Don't allow yourself or others to diminish your skills, abilities and worth in the job market. Encourage yourself, instead, to dream big. Once you've answered these questions here and researched the career options you're interested in, you can translate the information you've gathered so far into a career action plan. This will help you to break down your overall goal into smaller, more manageable steps following a specific timeline.

Update Your Resume. The question raised most often in this kind of situation is: "How do I write a resume when I don't have any recent paid job experience?" Your resume will include skills you already identified, accomplishments (such as a successful event you coordinated at your child's school), your roles and experiences volunteering and your education. Keep in mind that volunteer work is unpaid *work* and equally as valid as paid work in gaining experience. Validating this in your resume will help you develop the confidence to focus on skills you gained in any volunteer position(s).

You may also have questions along the lines of "Where can I get help?" "What books are out there?" "How do I write a resume?" "Who can help me write that resume?" "How do I prepare for an interview?" Please check out the *job search resources* listed at *www.bluestarcareers.com*, which address these particular questions.

Network. Now you're ready to network with people and assess where someone with your skill sets and experience fits into the marketplace. This step is crucial for people in your situation or for individuals undertaking a completely new career direction.

A way to "ease into" the networking approach may be to talk to people you've worked with in a volunteer capacity, asking them how they would describe your skills and if they would serve as a reference when you start interviewing. Once you've reached a comfort level with this networking approach, you can start meeting with other people in the community and asking for guidance in terms of career opportunities. Align those opportunities with your personal career goals, and before you know it, you'll be receiving calls inviting you to interview. But first, you need to believe in yourself. Then that confidence will come across in your interviews and you'll help would-be employers to see your potential.

Keep at It. Remember, the process of identifying a career opportunity has its ups and downs not just for you, but for every single applicant on the hunt. Prepare yourself mentally to confront some negatives and yet to find a way to maintain your confidence level. Your confidence will help you remain resilient if some of your efforts don't immediately materialize into a job offer and will help you better prepare for the interview.

Sleepwalking Through
Your Work Day?

Let a New Career Bring
You Back to Life

Do you feel as if you're sleepwalking through your usual work day? Do you find your job doesn't excite you anymore? Do you feel that you're probably too old, too stuck to make a change?

First of all, kudos to you for paying attention to your feelings about your current job before you become de-motivated and it affects your job performance. Secondly, it's not too late to identify your career passion and align yourself with a purpose. On average, people now change *careers* four to five times in their lives, not just jobs. If anything, you are "trendy."

Whether or not you have an idea of what it is you want to do professionally, here are a few suggestions on how you might start the process of regaining the drive that energizes your career:

Assess. Conduct a thorough assessment of your interests, abilities, personality and values. Following are a couple of suggestions for source material to get you started on your assessment.

- The Self-Directed Search by Dr. John Holland
        (*http://www.self-directed-search.com*)
- Career Alignment Profile®
        (*www.CAPassessment.com*)
- Selfcounseling.com
        (*http://selfcounseling.com/help
        /personalsuccess/personalvalues.html*)

- The book *Do What You Are: Discover the Perfect Career for You through the Secrets of Personality Type* by Paul D. Tieger and Barbara Barrone

- The book *What Color Is Your Parachute?* by Richard Nelson Bolles

- The book *Strengths Finder 2.0* by Tom Rath (*http://strengths.gallup.com/1104 40/About-StrengthsFinder-2.aspx*

More resources are listed *at www.bluestarcareers.com.*

Identify. Investigate career options that match your results and ultimately your passion. The resources listed above offer suggestions for career options that align with your individual assessment results. An additional excellent resource for exploring career options is *http://online.onetcenter.org.* This tool allows you to evaluate job families, its *(sic)* occupations and related skills and education, in addition to salary information and trends. You can even tailor your focus to a geographic area.

Research. Examine the top three choices in more depth, including education, skills, and experience required for this occupation and whether it's expected to need a growing number of workers in the next decade.

Analyze. Complete a gap analysis, identifying skills, knowledge, experience and education you may be missing.

Inquire. Conduct informational interviews with people in the occupations of your interest. Enlist the help of people in your network, e.g., friends, family and acquaintances, to identify individuals in these occupations. Or identify individuals by reading newspapers, trade journals or contacting the Chamber of Commerce or relevant professional organizations. When contacting the people you would like to interview, ensure that you clearly explain the purpose for requesting a meeting or phone appointment. Questions regarding the industry and occupation of interest will further aid you in evaluating your career options:

- Is this a rapidly growing industry overall? Which areas of this industry are experiencing a growth? Which areas are experiencing a decline?
- Which challenges do you expect in this industry in the next 5 years?
- From your perspective which organizations are leading this field?
- How do you stay up-to-date with the field? Which professional associations should I join?
- What are the duties you perform during a typical day in your occupation? Week? Month? Year?
- What do you enjoy about your job? What do you dislike about your job?
- What are the biggest challenges you encounter?
- What are the skills and competencies needed to be successful in this job?
- What educational degree or certificate do employers look for?
- What kind of work experience would employers look for in a job applicant?
- What was your career path like? Based on your experience what piece of advice would you give someone in my position?
- What are opportunities for advancement? Is an advanced degree needed?
- What types of technology are used and how are they used?
- Can you suggest any additional contacts or resources that may be valuable sources of information and guidance?

Choose. After careful consideration of factors that are important in your life, such as family needs, health, work environment, personal and work relationships, your desire to travel, your hoped-for income level, and growth opportunities within that industry, choose one career.

Plan or map. Translate your decision into a detailed career action plan, breaking down the overall goal into smaller, manageable steps with specific timelines. See the document for a *Sample Career Action Plan*.

Used by permission, Blue Star Careers, LLC.

How to Avoid Dueling Dialogue about Money

It probably won't surprise you that the subject most couples argue about is money. Given that we each grow up with different financial experiences, combining just about any two individuals' relationships with money has the potential for being a powder keg waiting to explode. However, it is possible to work together to achieve mutual financial goals if you keep a couple of things in mind.

Begin With Personal Financial Questions. Each of you should take a money attitude test. How did your parents handle money? Was it a frequent source of conflict? Were you worried about or afraid of money? When the two of you now talk about money, what words do you use? How do you handle money as a couple? Are you satisfied with that? What changes would you like to see, if any, in this area?

Talk Before the Fuse Is Lit. The saying *timing is everything* couldn't be more appropriate than when it comes to conversations about money. Set some time aside to talk about your answers to your financial quiz. Money situations that may have caused you stress in the past might be explainable as you begin to explore each other's past experiences and present perceptions around money. And as minor situations arise, sit down right away and talk. Waiting can only lead to the possibility of detonation.

Find Common Ground. Let's say you have different goals or different ideas on how to get there. First, find a common goal that is important to both of you. Brainstorm ideas of how to get there. Examine the possibility of each one. The attainment of the goal should take precedence. If you can't agree on the game plan, perhaps each of you could work on an idea and then meet regularly to talk about your progress.

Fit Allowances into the Budget. Keeping the peace in the financial household can be as simple as the two of you getting a set amount of money that you are not accountable for. This little bit of individual financial freedom can go a long way to keeping the family's finances on track.

Do What Works for You. Whether you choose a traditional approach to your family's money management, the autonomous approach or something in between, find the method that will allow you to achieve your financial goals with the least amount of fireworks.

So You Have An Idea –
Now What?

Have you ever come across an ad for a product or service that prompted you to say: "Hey! That was *my* idea!" So why didn't you act on that great idea? Didn't know where to start? If so, here is a step-by-step guide to bringing your product or service from imagination to reality.

Ask yourself some preliminary questions. Does your product or service meet a need or satisfy a want not currently being met? Does it solve a problem? Who is your customer? What do you think they would be willing to pay for your product or service?

Research: round one. Is your idea already in the marketplace? Use search engines such as Google to look for as many combinations of the concept you can think of. Look through catalogs. Check trade shows. Is your product or service less expensive, faster, easier to use, etc. than what is presently in the marketplace?

Research: round two. It's great to have a great idea, but can you make money at it? Is there a market for your idea? Who would you market to? How much does it cost to produce it? Again, the Internet is your friend. Search for the components to your product and price them. Check out *shapelock.com* where you can order microwavable pellets that can be molded into the shape of your gadget. Who is going to produce it, and what will that cost be? Explore the possibility of having a prototype made. At *thomas.net* you can enter the list of components of your product, and they will give you a list of factories that work with those components. Local machinist shops could also be a resource to make a prototype. When you know approximately how much it's going to cost to produce your product, add in postage and packaging materials.

So much for products. What about services? The initial financial outlay is generally less for service-based businesses. However, there are costs involved that need to be evaluated before you set up shop. Do your homework. How many businesses are out there offering the same services that you are considering? How can you make your services a little different, better, faster, less expensive? Apprentice yourself or volunteer in the area you're interested in to find out if the type of work/business is right for you. Also, as more service-based businesses go online, be aware there may be patent issues.

Whether your new business entails offering a service or launching a new product, the next question you need to ask yourself is: how much profit do you want to make per sale? There are a couple of schools of thought on this question. You could make less profit per sale and make more sales. Or you could make more profit on fewer sales. Once you've ball-parked your profit number, add that amount to the total product cost and look at that number. Do you think your customers would pay that price? If yes, then maybe you're on to something. If not, go back to the drawing board. Can you cut costs? Are you willing to make less profit? If the answers are no, it's possible that it doesn't make sense to move forward, and that's okay. Better to have spent a little time with paper, pencil and calculator to arrive at that conclusion than to have wasted months (or even longer) and a lot of money.

The first patent question. Do you need a patent? Can you put your product out in the marketplace quickly, and is its life short-lived? For example, the *Pet Rock*. When it hit the market, everyone had to have one. Then the craze was over almost as quickly as it had begun. A patent process can be lengthy and expensive. How does that fit into your profit margin and time frame? A good source for your patent questions is Sandra Etherton's *Let's Talk Patents*.

The second patent question. Is your product already patented? You can do some preliminary research yourself at the US Patent Office website *(www.uspto.gov)*, but before you activate the launch sequence – talk with a patent attorney. (For a list of patent attorneys go to: *www.uspto.gov.*) This is going to cost a little, but it could cost you a lot more if you skip this step.

Create a business plan. By this time you've run preliminary cost numbers, but here you get serious, and you may need some help. Through the Small Business Administration there is the Women's Business Center program (*www.sba.gov/womeninbusiness*) that provides training and counseling, usually at very low fees or free. SCORE (*www.score.org*) is a network of retired and working executives who freely share their expertise. They match the executive's area of expertise with that of the new entrepreneur. If there isn't a local chapter, a mentor can work with you online.

Market like your life depended on it. And the life of your business does. Email friends and family about your new business and ask them to pass it on. Network within the groups you're already involved in. Join business networking groups. Rent a booth at a trade show, local farmer's market or swap meet. Host a special event in your community. Team up with an organization or event. Have a contest. What can you do for free to get the word out? Give a workshop? Give out samples?

Secure Funding. For new businesses money is tough to come by. Babson College estimates that two-thirds of the average start-up capital comes from personal savings, family and friends.

Once you have a solid business plan and some cash flow, you can start to look elsewhere for other funding. You'll need to be specific as to amount and what you'll use the loan for.

- *Angel investors*. These investors will exchange capital for an ownership stake in your company.
- *Venture capital.* These firms provide money and management experience in return for an ownership stake.
- *SBA-guaranteed loans*. If you meet the criteria, Small Business Administration loans obtained through a commercial lender are a great source of funding. Their loan products vary in length and other terms based on specific purposes.

Staff it. Now you're cooking. If you haven't already, perhaps it's time to get some help. What type of help do you need? Where would you find that person? Schools? Clubs? Temp agencies offer personnel with a variety of experience, but also think outside the employment agency. Ask friends, family, colleagues, and acquaintances if they know anybody who could do what you're looking for. Once you've found someone, consider hiring them on a part-time or project basis. You can determine if they match your way of doing business and if you have enough work to support a full-time employee.

Checklist for Starting
A New Business

The Small Business Administration website has an excellent electronic assessment tool to help you determine your readiness to start your business. Check it out at: *www.sba.gov/assessmenttool.*

When you're ready, here is a step-by-step guide to establishing your new business.

- Meet with an accountant to determine what type of business entity would best suit you and your business. (See the article on *Business Entity Comparison.*)
- Pick a business entity.
- Consult with an attorney or research the laws governing the creation, ownership and operation of the entity.
- Execute the agreement.
- File with state for certificate of assumed name (DBA).
- Obtain a Federal Employer Identification Number (EIN). Go to *www.irs.gov*, type in "EIN" in the search box located in the upper right corner of the website, then click on "Apply for an Employer Identification Number" online. Also, you can call the Internal Revenue Service at 800-829-4933 to obtain an EIN over the phone.
- File incorporation, limited liability company (LLC) or partnership documents with the state.
- Obtain state and local identification numbers for sales tax and payroll reports.
- Obtain local/city/county business licenses and permits.
- Establish a business checking account.
- Fund the entity.
- Conduct necessary meetings and elect a Board of Directors.
- Create the books.
- Contact insurance professionals to obtain the necessary liability and professional coverage.

- Review wills and estate plans of owners.
- Hire employees.
- Start operations.

Business Entity Comparison

The two main areas of consideration when choosing a type of business entity are legal and taxation. For legal purposes, do you need to protect your assets from judgments that may arise from lawsuits against your company? Is it important to you that your business continues if you no longer actively participate in it? Because each entity is taxed differently, it is important to know how the business income will be taxed.

The decisions you make at the onset of your business can have long-term implications, so you should consider consulting with an attorney and accountant or perform sufficient research in order to make an informed decision.

The following is a brief description of the various types of entities. Consider these a starting point in your decision-making process as opposed to a sole source of information about business entities.

Sole Proprietorship. As in Marla's case, many small businesses start off as sole proprietorships because they are the easiest and least expensive to form. These are usually a one-person operation where the owner performs all the duties of running the business and assumes all the liabilities associated with the business. Setting up this type of entity is very straightforward. There is no formation paperwork to complete as there is for corporations, partnerships and LLCs. For tax purposes, appropriate forms reporting the business activities are attached to your personal returns, so no separate returns are necessary.

Some of the disadvantages to sole proprietorships are that the owner has unlimited liability, and both personal and business assets can be at risk. Also, business financing may be more challenging for sole proprietorships, and there is no way to bring in outside capital contributors. As a result, owners have to utilize personal funds and credit sources. Unlike corporations or partnerships, there is no business continuation provision, which means that the business ceases when the owner dies.

Limited Liability Company (LLC). These legal entities are formed under state law and are designed to provide the limited personal liability feature of a corporation and the tax efficiencies and operational flexibility of other entity structures. Single-member LLCs are usually treated as disregarded entities and taxed directly to their owner, such as in the case of a sole proprietor or rental property, or you can choose to be taxed as a corporation. An LLC with two or more members is generally classified as a partnership for tax purposes unless you elect to be taxed as a corporation. The main advantage to this type of structure is that you do not have to observe corporate formalities such as annual meetings and election of officers. The main disadvantage is the inconsistent treatment between states of this type of structure.

Partnership. Two or more persons agree to own and operate a business. Profits and losses are shared and reported directly on the partners' personal tax returns by way of a partnership tax return. These entities are relatively easy to establish. However, you should invest time in developing the partnership agreement, which should cover such areas as: how profits/losses are to be divided; who is responsible for decision-making; how disputes will be resolved; how new partners will be admitted and existing partners be bought out; and how dissolution will take place. The main disadvantage to partnerships is there is unlimited personal liability for the general partners.

Corporation. This business entity carries its own legal status, sole and separate from its owners, the shareholders. It can be taxed or sued and can enter into contracts. Some of the advantages to this choice of business entity are that the corporation has a life of its own, and a transfer of ownership is easy. Liability rests primarily with the corporation, not its shareholders. Some of the disadvantages are that organizing a corporation is difficult, and it must comply with federal and state regulations. Incorporating may result in higher overall taxes. The corporation must hold periodic meetings and keep minutes.

Subchapter S Corporation. A corporation can make a tax election (through IRS Form 2553) that enables the shareholder to treat earnings and profits as distributions and have them pass through to their personal tax return. This type of corporation is limited to domestic corporations with only one class of stock and less than 100 shareholders, as long as no shareholder is another corporation. Employee-shareholders must pay themselves a "reasonable" wage based on local compensation for similar work. Because this is an election of a corporation, advantages and disadvantages are similar to those of corporations except that the double taxation issue arising from the payout of dividends does not apply to S corporations.

There are a lot of factors to consider in your choice for a business entity and well worth the time to explore each one with your advisors.

Increasing Your Net Worth
Bottom Line

There are two ways to increase your net worth: increase the assets or decrease the liabilities. The characters have already discussed the primary techniques to accomplish this goal.

Increase Your Assets

Take advantage of your employer's retirement plan matching, plus contribute as much as you can above the match amount.

Establish an emergency fund of between three and six months of income in a savings or money market account. Rates for these types of accounts are typically low because the money is easily accessible. Find the highest rate you can.

Target the areas on the Balance Sheet which have the potential to appreciate in value over time and/or generate income, such as investments, income-producing real estate, retirement accounts, and cash/savings.

Decrease Your Liabilities

Reduce your liabilities by paying off credit cards and car loans.

Limit spending in areas such as furniture, cars, and personal property, which tend to be purchased through the use of financing. In addition to minimizing your liabilities, the less spent on property which generally depreciates in value, the more money you'll have to invest in property which may have the potential to increase in value.

Open Mind for Opportunity

Everyone can do something of value that can be marketed, that can generate income. Everybody has a story to tell that could help someone else, a service to offer that could benefit someone or a product someone could use. How do you discover your hidden treasure?

Figure out what interests you. In Jade's case, she grew up rehabbing houses with her dad. She likes breathing new life into old buildings, recycling and reusing, and recognizes the financial rewards of real estate. Marla enjoys decorating and creating a nice home for her family. She connected a couple of dots to come up with a saleable product. Rita probably wouldn't have imagined herself in a management position at SterTechCo while her husband was alive, but when she learned about the state of the company he had founded and worked so hard to maintain, she jumped at the opportunity to do whatever she could to save it.

Look around you. Jade deviated from her usual drive to work and found herself stuck in traffic long enough to notice the Atwood house. There are opportunities everywhere if you take the time to look for them. In fact, let's do a quick exercise. Look around you and pick an object. What could be done to it to make it better? Cheaper? What could be combined with it or removed from it to create a new product? What if it was smaller or bigger? What don't you like about it? How could you make it more desirable, more functional? Could it be made more (or less) gender-specific to open it up to a new customer pool?

Think. Turn off the television, talk radio and the computer. Put down the magazine and the newspaper. Give yourself a break from the barrage of visual and audio stimulation. Take a walk. Do the dishes. Pet the dog. And think. About anything. The universe. Your navel. The meaning of life. What's bugging you. Write about it, if you'd like. You've probably been thinking the same thoughts for years now. Have some new ones. You may find one that's worth a million dollars.

Or don't think. And see what pops into your mind. Have you ever tried to think of someone's name, and it was only after you quit thinking about it, you remember it? That's because the name was stored in your subconscious, and that part of the brain has a tough time communicating with you when you're talking to yourself. Find a quiet spot, sit in a comfortable position and close your eyes. Allow your conscious mind to settle into silence and listen to what your subconscious has to say.

Keep an idea diary. Set an intention that you want to come up with at least one idea for a new product or service every day. Keep a small spiral notebook handy and write them down as they come to you. And come they will. Then begin to evaluate them. See the article: *So You Have an Idea – Now What?*

How to Buy a House – From Dream to Reality

If purchasing a home is your dream, you've got lots of company. The vision is shared by millions of Americans. And if you didn't know where to start, you've come to the right place. The following is a step-by-step guide from dream to reality.

Get pre-prequalified/pre-approved. The first part of your interaction with a lender will give you a price range in which you would tentatively qualify based on your annual income. Add that to your down payment, and you will arrive at the purchase price of your home. (For loan parameters, see the article entitled *Residential and Commercial Lending*.) As you move through the home-buying process, you will have to supply documents that verify your income including pay stubs, tax returns and bank account statements, and liabilities such as auto loan and credit card balances and monthly payments.

Pick a couple of areas you like. Drive around neighborhoods you would like to live in and write down addresses of houses shown for sale. Most cities have a Multiple Listing Service (MLS) that is accessible by the general public through the Internet. In addition to the asking price, the listing will give you a host of valuable information and, many times, pictures of the property. If you don't have access to the Internet, or if MLS is not available in your area, a real estate agent can provide listing information.

Choose an agent. Especially first-time homebuyers, but everyone, can benefit from the services of a good real estate agent. Ask friends and family for recommendations. Notice whose name appears most often on the signs in neighborhoods you are interested in. Often realtors focus their efforts and specialize in certain areas, which can be invaluable to homebuyers. Interview a couple of agents to find one you feel will do the best job.

Make a list of wants and needs. This list will give your agent an idea what amenities are most important to you. Then based on purchase price and desired area, together you can decide which ones to focus on.

Take a look around. Once you and your agent have come up with a list of houses that meet your criteria, you will begin the actual house hunting. These walk-throughs also give the realtor a better idea of exactly what you're looking for. If you don't happen to find your new home on the first trip together, your agent can preview other properties and select those to show you that will most closely match your specific wants and needs.

Look again. Once you've pretty much decided on a house, take a second look before making an offer. Put on your *can-I-see-myself-living-here* glasses and decide if it still works for you.

Make an offer. You make an offer to purchase a house through a contract, which spells out the specifics of the deal. In addition to the purchase price, this document contains such details as what personal property will convey with the real property, the closing date, the down payment amount, and the deadline by which to respond, etc. If the seller accepts your offer, congratulations. What is more likely is that the seller will counter-offer. Where you go from there depends on a host of different factors such as the seller's motivation and the local real estate market. Your real estate agent will be an excellent guide through this process.

Work to close the loan. After providing the mortgage broker with a copy of the sales contract, work with the lender to ensure you meet the conditions required for the closing of the loan.

Have an inspection done. You will want to make sure you have an inspection performed by a qualified home inspector. These professionals are trained to find flaws in the construction of the home that may not be obvious to the naked eye, such as electrical or plumbing issues.

Sign the papers. Once the inspection report has come back clean, it's time to close. During the closing you hand over the down payment and sign documents transferring the property to you, as well as the loan documents. After the title has been recorded, you will receive the keys to your new home.

Congratulations!

Residential and Commercial Lending

No doubt the mortgage fallout has changed the world of lending. The good news is that lenders have money to loan and want to lend it out. The bad news is that it's not as easy to get as it was at one time.

What is the residential or commercial lender looking for from a borrower? What are the general parameters for these loans?

One important area for both types of loans is the relationship with your lender and/or bank. If you are a good customer, your chances of getting a loan with them can be enhanced. Being a "good" customer can take on different definitions, but it generally means being a customer for over three years, using multiple services beyond a checking account and having some type of borrowing history. Also, if the lending decision could go either way, the relationship could tip the scale in your favor.

Residentially speaking. The rules for residential lending apply to properties up to and including four houses on one site, commonly referred to as a four-plex. Generally, the down payment for residential loans is between five and ten percent, and the term is usually thirty years. Appraisal fees run around $250, and the underwriting fee (assessed by the lender to write the loan) is about one percent of the loan amount. Other significant, but optional, fees are used to reduce or "buy down" the interest rates.

If the house is going to be your primary residence (owner-occupied), the lender is oftentimes permitted to make concessions for the credit approval based on house value, sufficient wage/cash flow to support repayment, credit scores and bank statements. These loans are personal, so the approval is all about the buyer's financials. In the case of rental property, mortgage brokers will include rental income and expenses in the total income available to make the loan payment, but in the end, the decision to loan lies with the borrower's ability to repay, and sometimes without relying on the future rental income.

Commercially speaking. Commercial properties include residential dwellings of five or more units and buildings used for office, retail and industrial purposes.

There are two types of commercial loans: conventional and Small Business Association (SBA) commercial. Generally, the down payment for a conventional loan is between twenty and twenty-five percent, whereas SBA loans require between ten and fifteen percent. In either case the loan amount is amortized up to twenty-five years for the conventional and up to thirty years for the SBA. Unlike residential loans where the interest rate can remain the same throughout the loan period, the interest rate on commercial loans is generally shorter, fixed for only ten years at which time the rate could be reset to current market rates. Also, appraisal fees are substantially higher – locally, they run around $3,500. The underwriting fee for a conventional commercial loan usually runs approximately one percent of the loan amount, but is negotiable. SBA fees are set by the Federal Government and vary depending on the type of loan, e.g., equipment, real estate or acquisition. The rate range is 1.5%-3% of the loan amount.

Whereas on the residential side the focus is on the borrower's personal financials, for commercial loans heavy emphasis is placed on the business plan and leases. Three sources of repayment are identified.

- *Cash flow from the property or main business*. Ideally the property or business supports the loan payment without dipping into owners' income or reserves.

- Sale or liquidation of the collateral. Some discount on the value is applied in case a rapid sale is needed.

- *Owners' assets and other income*.

In the underwriting process cash flow is analyzed, and ratios are applied similar to what Paul explained to Jade.

Alternative Financing for Real Estate

Jade's financial ratios didn't meet the bank's criteria for either a residential or commercial loan, and she didn't have the money for the down payment, but driven by experience in real estate and her comfort level with accepting that level of risk, she looked for an alternative way to buy and finance the Atwood house. Here are descriptions of several alternative financing options for real estate.

Seller-financing. If the seller has substantial equity in the property, the seller acts as the bank for any or all of the financing to the buyer. Documents are prepared outlining the terms and conditions of the note, including the amount of the note, payment amount, interest rate and length of the loan.

Money partners. There are people who like investing in real estate but have no desire to perform the "hands on" part of finding and managing property. If you like the operational part of real estate investment, this type of arrangement might work for you. As true partners, it is recommended you form a partnership by way of a partnership agreement, spelling out the specifics of your arrangement, e.g., percentage of ownership, scope of responsibilities, division of management, share of income and losses, etc.

Lease to own. In this situation you would enter into an agreement with the seller to lease the property for a specified period of time, and you would be given credit, when you purchase the property, for a portion of the lease payment. The agreement would also contain an agreed-upon purchase price. This arrangement gives you the option to purchase the property, not an obligation.

Family and friends. Mixing family and finances can turn out badly. But if you treat them as you would any other investor, including signed notes with clear-cut consequences, this arrangement could be a win-win for both sides. Prove to them how they're going to get a good rate of return and when they will get their money back.

Hard money lenders. These investors loan money for short periods of time (usually for less than six months) at a high rate of return. Since these notes are private arrangements, you can oftentimes receive the necessary funds within days of the request. This type of loan is an excellent source of funds in situations when time is of the essence, when permanent financing is perhaps unnecessary, or when traditional lenders are unable to fund a loan.

Trade/barter. As Jade discovered, sometimes a situation presents itself where an exchange of services could be a source of funds. Even though there are tax consequences to barter income, the benefit of this option is that you don't have to come up with cash.

These are but a few ideas. There are several good books devoted to this subject alone, including those by Robert Allen and many written on the general subject of real estate. Check out your local library and bookstores to find the ones that work for you.

Good Tenants – How to Find Them and How to Keep Them

Good tenants are the key to successful rental property. You want them to take care of your property as though it was their own, pay you on time, and leave the property in the same shape in which they found it. Right? So how do you find the perfect tenant? And then how do you keep them?

Put your best foot forward. The first step in finding a good tenant is to offer a good-looking property. Make sure everything sparkles on the inside and is immaculate on the outside.

When meeting with prospective tenants, be professional. After all, this is your business and the property your product. Treat them with the same respect you expect when purchasing products and services.

Advertise. The Internet is a great place to advertise. You can post your ad with pictures on *craigslist.com* at no cost. Spend some time on your ad copy. Make sure it contains your property's best characteristics. Put a sign in the front yard. Spread the word among friends and family. What schools or businesses surround your property which may allow you to post an ad on their bulletin boards?

Show. Arrive a little early for the appointment to make sure everything is just right. Point out the property's features and specify which expenses are included in the rent, such as water, trash collection fees, etc. As your prospective tenants leave, give them a standard rental application. (Use "rental application" to search for one on the Internet.) Make sure it contains a clause that gives permission to release information. You'll need that when you verify the information they provide.

Verify. Once you have a completed rental application check the information, including calling references, contacting their previous landlord, and verifying employment history. Request recent paystubs and

Form 1099s to confirm income.

Do a credit report. Ask for a nonrefundable application fee to cover this expense. If the prospective tenant has had difficulty in paying bills in the past, you don't want to be added to the list. Also, by charging this fee, you'll know they are serious.

Maintain. Maintain the property by keeping everything in good working order and looking nice. And maintain a good relationship with your tenants by being responsive and communicative. The end result will be a win-win for both you and your tenant.

LaVergne, TN USA
17 August 2010
193640LV00002B/2/P